The Choral Conductor's Aural Tutor

**Other resources by James Jordan
available from GIA Publications, Inc.**

Evoking Sound: The Choral Warm-Up
(Core Vocal Exercises)
(G-6397)

The Choral Warm-Up Accompanist Supplement with Accompaniment CD
(G-6397A)

The Choral Warm-Up Index Card Pack
(G-6397I)

Ear Training Immersion Exercises for Choirs
(G-6429)

Choral Ensemble Intonation: Methods, Procedures, and Exercises
with Matthew Mehaffey
(G-5527T)

Choral Ensemble Intonation: Teaching Procedures Video
(VHS-500)

Evoking Sound
(G-4257)

Evoking Sound Video: Body Mapping Principles and
Basic Conducting Technique
with Heather Buchanan
(DVD-530)

The Musician's Soul
(G-5095)

The Musician's Spirit
(G-5866)

The Musician's Walk: An Ethical Labyrinth
(G-6734)

EVOKING SOUND

The Choral Conductor's Aural Tutor

TRAINING THE EAR TO
DIAGNOSE VOCAL PROBLEMS

A Companion to *The Choral Warm-Up*

James Jordan

SUPPLEMENTAL RESOURCES

Two Aural Study CDs
with The Westminster Williamson Voices
of Westminster Choir College of Rider University
and The Pennsbury High School Chamber Choir

Marilyn Shenenberger, Accompanist
James Jordan, Conductor

GIA Publications, Inc.
Chicago

Evoking Sound
The Choral Conductor's Aural Tutor: Training the Ear to Diagnose Vocal Problems
A Companion to *The Choral Warm-Up*
James Jordan

Layout: Joel A. Sibick

GIA Publications, Inc.
7404 S. Mason Ave., Chicago 60638
Copyright © 2006 GIA Publications, Inc.
All rights reserved.
Printed in the United States of America

G-6905
ISBN-10: 1-57999-600-0
ISBN-13: 978-1-57999-600-0

www.giamusic.com

Dedicated to
Marilyn Shenenberger

Few conductors could be as fortunate to have as their colleague and musical partner an accompanist with the musical and pedagogical gifts of Marilyn Shenenberger. Her thought, musicianship, and humanness are transforming the choral accompanist's role in the choral rehearsal.

a n d

To my conducting students at the Westminster Choir College of Rider University and music education students at West Chester University for whom these materials were developed to make their way into this profession a bit easier.

"Loyalty to a petrified opinion never yet broke a chain
or freed a human soul."

—Mark Twain

CONTENTS

Preface xi
BEFORE YOU BEGIN: PRETEST xv
Use of Headphones or Earphones to Study xvi
Accompaniment Playing Suggestions and Accompaniments
    without Voices xvi
Using the Recommended Listening List for Further
    Analysis and Vocal Study xvii

SECTION I

INTRODUCTION AND PURPOSE 1
Importance of Error Detection for Conductors 4
The Selection of Aural Models for These Recordings 5
Philosophical Design of the Tutorial CD and Selection of Exercises 5
Core Aural Pedagogical Issues 6
Seat the Choir to Maximize Your Ability to Hear and Detect Problems
    within the Ensemble 7
Further Discussion of the Alto-in-Front Seating Arrangement 8
The Conductor's Ear: How Do We Really Hear? 10
Use of the Tutorial CDs 11
Consistency of Conducting Gestures 11
All Conducting Gestures Should Stay "Down" When the Choir
    Sings Upward on Leaping Passages 12
Hearing Off-the-Breath Singing 12
Shortening the Core Alignment of the Body 13
An Inability to "Release" the Gesture after the Ictus 14
A Hand Position Always Parallel to the Floor? 15

SECTION TWO:

DEVELOPING ANALYTICAL LISTENING SKILLS 17

Reprioritize Your Listening Skills: How to Develop
    Pedagogical Listening 19
Audiation and Awareness 20
Setting Audiational Priorities 23
Familiar versus Unfamiliar 23
Acquisition of Model Vocal Sounds through Audiational Study
    by the Conductor 24
Monitoring Sound versus an Awareness of Sound 24
Understanding and Developing Timbre Acuity: Foreground
    versus Background 25

SECTION THREE

HOW DO YOU HEAR? 27

How Do We Hear? Implications of the Thought of Alfred A. Tomatis
    for Conductors 29
The Functioning of the Ear 31
Right Ear Dominance in Vocal Production and Listening: Acquiring
    More Aural Acuity 32
Establishing a Listening Posture for the Ear 34

SECTION FOUR

IDENTIFYING ASPECTS OF TIMBRE 35

What Is Choral Timbre? 37
Be Aware of Your Timbre Defaults 37
Aural Models Acquired Outside This Tutor 38
Posttest Evaluation 38
The Role of the Accompanist 39
Essentials of Vocal Listening for the Conductor: Root Problems 39
Hearing Pitch and Rhythm: Score Preparation Is the Key 40
On-the-Breath Singing 40
Unspacious, High Larynx Singing 41

Sounds that Are Not High and Forward 41
Help for Hearing Subtleties of Vocal Sound: Color 42
Omnipresent Necessity for Musical Line: Hearing Musical Line 43
Listening for Issues of Rhythmic Energy and Clarity 44
Aggressiveness in Sound 44

SECTION FIVE

THE CONDUCTOR'S AURAL WORKBOOK 47
Introduction 49
Core Vocal Exercises: Model Exercises and Embedded Problems 56
Issues of Register Breaks: A Problem that Masks Other Problems 57
Accuracy of Language When Analyzing Aural Examples 58
The Tutorial Exercises: Instructions 59
CD 1: The Westminster Williamson Voices 61
Accompaniment Suggestions: Marilyn Shenenberger 61
Exercises and Notebook for The Westminster Williamson Voices 62
CD 2: The Pennsbury High School Chamber Choir 77
Accompaniment Suggestions: Marilyn Shenenberger 77
Exercises and Notebook for The Pennsbury Chamber Choir 78

SECTION SIX

PRETESTS AND POSTTESTS 93
Instructions (CD 1, Track 57) 95
Pretest (Exam One) 96
Pretest (Exam Two) 99
Pretest (Exam Three) 102
Posttest (Exam One) 105
Posttest (Exam Two) 108
Posttest (Exam Three) 111
Pretest and Posttest Answers 114

SECTION SEVEN

EXPANDING YOUR ABILITY TO HEAR CHORAL TEXTURES AND COLORS 117

Gaining More Listening Experiences for Choral Color: Hearing
    Resonances 119
Setting Your Listening Priorities 119
Hearing Musical Styles: Vocalic Flow and Mode 119
Gaining the Ability to Hear the Colors of the Modes 121
The Role of Visualization of Color and Its Effects upon Choral Sound .121
The Crayola School of Texture Education 123
Create an Inspiration Board or Collage for Pieces You Conduct 124
Tall and Narrow versus Rounder Resonances:
    Avoid Bright versus Dark 124

SECTION EIGHT

RECOMMENDED LISTENING LIST FOR FURTHER AURAL ANALYSIS AND COLOR STUDY 127

Recommended Listening List for Further Aural
    Analysis and Color Study 129
Before You Listen: The Sound Concept of
    The Westminster Williamson Voices 129
Recommended Track Listening from Resource Recordings
    to *Teaching Music through Performance in Choir, Volume 1* 131
Supplementary Recordings Recommended for
    Further Aural Study 136
Other Suggested Recordings 142

Resources 143
Biographies 145

Preface

From the beginning of my musical life, I always marveled at the finest conductors and their ability to mysteriously diagnose issues of *sound* and *color* within an ensemble.

The easiest skill for a conductor to develop, in my opinion, is the identification of pitch and rhythm errors. Much conducting pedagogy revolves around teaching the techniques of pitch and rhythm error detection. However, I observed many years ago that the best conductors do not waste valuable rehearsal time correcting pitches and rhythms. Instead, these conductors are very skillful in leading the ensemble to be responsible for accurate notes and rhythms. Because of that fascination, Matthew Mehaffey, Marilyn Shenenberger, and I have developed a system of choral ensemble solfege that does just that: it empowers the ensemble to be responsible for the correct and accurate performance of both pitches and rhythms. Left to their own devices, ensembles can be quite effective in hearing and fixing pitch and rhythm problems if they are taught listening skills. However, it is much more difficult to approach the matter of diagnostic vocal listening for conductors, which is a type of "vocal technique ear training."

Vocal techniques and ear training for choral conductors are fascinating topics for me. However, my work is not meant to replace the ear training that is already done so well by theory and Kodály teachers. I have long believed that great studio voice teachers are not always ones who necessarily sing the best (although most of them do!), but rather are those who have finely developed pedagogical ears. The great voice teacher hears the subtlest nuance in each voice he or she teaches. That diagnostic skill, coupled with a pedagogical persistence, is what makes for great voice teaching.

Likewise, many of the great choral minds of the last fifty years that I have observed have the same diagnostic skills as great voice teachers. My models? Wilhelm Ehmann, Paul Salamunovich, Sabine Horstmann, Frauke Haasemann, Constantina Tsolainou, Robert E. Page, and Elaine Brown. All seem to have both an intuitive and perceptive gift with regard to the vocal health of the ensemble sound. It is also clear to me that they have somehow reprioritized their ensemble hearing. Issues of vocal health, the color of the sound, and the human content of the sound had, at times, a higher priority on the ladder of listening than the easier and more obvious elements of pitch and rhythm.

There is another more serious danger when one does not listen on several levels. A well-known conductor I have observed many times prides himself in "fixing the pitch immediately." While that is an impressive skill in itself, a wrong or inaccurate pitch may be caused by a vocal problem. In many situations, fixing the pitch alone without finding the root of the problem will cause that problem to rear its ugly head again and again. Pitch problems are caused either by the singers' unfamiliarity with the harmonic landscape they are immersed in or by poor vocal technique.

My belief is that fundamental vocal technique problems cause a chain reaction of other problems within the ensemble. If the conductor remains aurally vigilant concerning basic issues of vocal technique, many other problems that plague ensembles simply do not appear.

The best conductors understand that matters of accurate pitch and rhythm have their roots in correct singing. Inaccurate pitches and rhythms are symptoms, and the cause lies in an alloy of technique melded with spirit. These conductors also seemed to realize that focusing only on pitch and rhythm yields few long-term benefits to ensemble health. While correcting pitch is an acceptable and necessary strategy in instrumental music, it is a flawed approach in choral music. When conductors "fix pitch," singers unknowingly manipulate their singing technique to achieve the adjustment in pitch demanded by the conductor. This always results in a restricted, tight sound with less color potential than a freely produced vocal sound.

This book provides young conductors with a jump start on the process of diagnostic vocal listening as well as attempts to reprioritize the listening of more experienced conductors and to share my information and ideas concerning vocal ensemble health. This is a first step and is by no means all-inclusive; the content of the text is obviously fraught with my own bias! Nonetheless, I believe that the essentials presented here can form the basis for a renewed sense of listening to how ensembles sing. Once the ability to analyze and diagnose vocal sound is in place, pedagogical solutions are much more obvious and efficient.

While recognition of problems within a choral sound is essential, this ability can only be built through the careful development of the audiational skills of the conductor. Being able to hear sound without the sound being physically present is the basis by which sound can accurately be compared to a standard in our minds' ear, and that is the skill this volume attempts to develop and nurture.

—James Jordan

Before You Begin: Pretest

Before you begin studying choral sound, take a pretest to determine how well you hear. Go to page 95 and load CD 1, track 57. Complete and score Exam One and Exam Two, which should be taken consecutively. Follow the scoring procedure in the Pretest and Posttest Answers section beginning on page 114.

When you interpret your results, look for two trends. First, record the number of incorrect answers for each test. If there is a wide variance or difference between scores, you can interpret that discrepancy as an inconsistency in your ability to diagnose vocal problems. You should study the entire tutorial in great detail and then retest yourself at the end of your study of one or both CDs. Second, if there is little or no difference in your scores, it may be interpreted that you come to this aural tutor with some listening skills in place. What you need to do in this case is list the categories of answers where you had incorrect responses to the items and focus your aural study on those tracks that deal with the problems you missed.

You may also wish to make copies of the unanswered tests for future use. It has been my experience that it will take several repeated studies of this material to truly master it with depth and consistency over a period of time. I must also caution you to consider that retention of this ability is only maintained with constant reinforcement and repetition of study. *Do not become discouraged if you continue to score low on the retest exams.* Remember that aural skill development requires both time and patience. Listening skills develop over time and may not improve after only a two-hour investment in study.

Also know that while you may believe you are developing a very specific hearing ability, you are, in fact, developing an all-inclusive listening awareness concerning choral sound. The listening ear often plays aural tricks on us. Until you develop an ability to vividly fantasize about the color of the sound, you probably will have some challenges in discriminating between and among different problems. Remember, the key to the use of this tutor and your aural growth as a conductor is repeated hearings of each study item; this means listening to the correct performance followed by a silence for audiation, followed immediately by the incorrect performance. There will be limited benefits and growth if you merely listen to all of the exercises from beginning to end. Moreover, little if any aural growth will take place if you do not make notes about the sounds you hear in the workbook section of this tutor.

Use of Headphones or Earphones to Study

It is important to use either headphones or earphones when using the tutorial CDs. Listening through a system in a room invites the interference of extraneous noises and will most certainly break your concentration. In order to develop in-depth listening skills, your listening experience needs to be in the controlled environment of the headphone world! Personally, I favor the *Bose Acoustic Noise Canceling Headphones* that, with the touch of a switch, eliminate all extraneous noises from your environment while you are listening. However, earbud listening devices such as those that come standard with most iPods are very acceptable. What is important to remember here is to always listen with headphones of some type.

Accompaniment Playing Suggestions and Accompaniments without Voices

The enclosed CDs contain my playing suggestions along with those by Marilyn Shenenberger, followed by the accompaniments alone. These accompaniments without voices help conductors listen to the accompaniments separately to anchor issues of musical line, musical motion, and elements of tension and release. It is important to listen to these exercises alone to absorb musical details. While this workbook's major objective is to tutor one to hear issues regarding vocal technique, it is also important to be able to hear musical issues within the accompaniments. The aural skills of the conductor rest on his or her ability to be aurally aware of all musical elements. Remember that informed pedagogical listening is a process of maintaining a general awareness, not a specific focus on any particular element. To develop that all-encompassing aural awareness, one must study, through listening, each of the specific elements of musical texture.

Using the Recommended Listening List for Further Analysis and Vocal Study

Finally, when you achieve a score of thirteen or better on the posttest, I would encourage you to then invest considerable time listening to many of the recordings suggested on the *Recommended Listening List for Further Aural Analysis and Color Study* found at the back of this volume. Begin, however, with the annotated listening guide to the tracks for *Teaching Music through Performance in Choir, Vol.1* (3-CD set, GIA CD-650) on page 131. As an extra feature in this tutor, some recordings to begin this process are included on each CD. These recordings and the recordings on the recommended list represent a wide variety of choral sounds and musicological styles. Many of the recordings come with annotations and suggestions for their use. I would suggest study of these recordings in tandem with preparations of performances with your choir. For example, if you were preparing a performance of the Duruflé *Requiem*, I would listen to performances suggested on this list in great detail before you begin any rehearsal on that work. While this list is not exhaustive, it does provide a starting point for the further development of your ability to hear subtle variations in choral sound.

SECTION ONE
INTRODUCTION AND PURPOSE

Section One: Introduction and Purpose

> Now, no one would deny that a most important part of good vocalism is vocal "line." What we mean by that is unanimity of vocal color through the widest possible range of pitch and dynamics. At its best, "vocal line" issues in a noble legato sound so pleasing and moving that stringed instruments attempt to imitate it by sliding with the left hand on the finger-board, rather than by leaping with fingers to successive pitches. (p. 110)
> —Robert Shaw
> *The Robert Shaw Reader*

There is a bit of folklore passed among veteran teachers of conducting that anyone who can hear can be taught to conduct. Another way of viewing the idea is that anyone who hears can eventually become a skilled conductor. There is some truth in both those statements. However, the statements also, beneath the surface, imply that either a person hears or they don't and that hearing, or more precisely, listening, cannot be taught.

While it may be a difficult thing to teach, perhaps aware listening can be taught. Listening for pitches and rhythms is an easy skill to teach. I believe the challenge is to teach a type of listening that is inclusive rather than exclusive, i.e., listening in such a way as to focus only on specific musical details. However, listening for aspects of choral texture and color and teaching how to do that can be a bit more challenging. While many of us acknowledge the difficulty of that pedagogical challenge, there are relatively few known approaches that have been developed to teach these skills if they are not already present in the conductor.

Along those lines, another persistent problem in the training of conductors and teachers of choral ensembles is how to provide conductors and teachers with aural examples to develop "diagnostic ears." The challenge is to teach conductors to hear vocal problems in an actual rehearsal. In fact, before developing this book, I found it difficult, if not impossible, to explain this skill to both young and old conductors alike.

> Knowing that we learn what something is by learning what it is not is the central pedagogical principle of this tutorial and CD.

One of the struggles I have had in many summer and academic-year courses is that it is one thing to teach conductors the method of choral ensemble vocal training and the associated teaching techniques and exercises, but it is another to provide aural models for further training. It has long been my desire to provide a CD with not only the correct vocal modeling by a choral ensemble but examples with embedded problems.

Correctly sung examples appear immediately before incorrectly sung examples. In this way, conductors immediately can aurally juxtapose a correct performance with an exercise that has problems so as to train their ears to critically hear technical vocal faults in a choral ensemble. Also, keep in mind that the material presented here is a starting point for your diagnostic listening study. My desire is to present broad and general vocal concepts important to build a strong, pedagogically rooted "conductor's ear."

Importance of Error Detection for Conductors

By far, it is much more difficult to diagnose vocal problems within a vocal ensemble than in a voice lesson. First, the most serious danger is that most vocal problems start rather insidiously with one or two voices within a choral ensemble. Over a period of time, the number singing incorrectly multiplies exponentially if the conductor's diagnostic ears are not engaged. One of the serious issues I have found with many conductors is that they focus on pitch and rhythm errors almost exclusively. Some other conductors also focus on musical line, believing that it is the root of all vocal ills. I happen to disagree.

> The conductor's most important line of defense is the ability to discriminate between and among various problems concerning vocal technique.

The systemic root problem of several other choral ensemble difficulties lies with vocal technique problems. To continually correct and adjust pitch issues without addressing vocal placement and vocal resonance issues damages voices in the long run. An inability to hear on-the-breath singing as opposed to off-the-breath singing creates both pitch problems and serious resonance issues, not to mention the pressure and strain it places upon the vocal mechanism.

---

1. For a comprehensive approach to improving intonation in the choral ensemble, the reader is encouraged to study two books available from GIA Publications: *Choral Ensemble Intonation: Methods, Procedures, and Exercises* by James Jordan and Matthew Mehaffey and *Ear Training Immersion Exercises for Choirs* by James Jordan and Marilyn Shenenberger.

Elements of pitch and rhythm (right vs. wrong pitch and rhythm) must be addressed and taught separately via the use of solfege and appropriate accompanying techniques.[1] In fact, it is my belief that the conductor must be constantly vigilant concerning the health of the sound within the vocal ensemble apart from other musical issues of concern. In many respects, one could certainly argue that vocal technique ills are at the root of other problems that mask themselves as musical problems.

The Selection of Aural Models for These Recordings

When asked in workshops, "Do these techniques in *The Choral Warm-Up* work with any age choir?" I always answer yes! Everyone would agree that good vocal technique is good vocal technique whether it is for children or adults. The difficulty lies in the fact that the quality of the sound of a choral ensemble varies from age to age. Hence, the same vocal problem may sound slightly different depending on both the age and the experience of the singers. I provide two aural models for conductors to begin their vocal ear-training course: a college choir and a high school choir. In addition, I suggest recordings for further study that represent singing in young choirs at the highest levels.

Philosophical Design of the Tutorial CD and Selection of Exercises

The original intent was to record all twenty-four *Core Vocal Exercises* contained in *The Choral Warm-Up*. However, it seemed both redundant and unnecessary to record several exercises that share a similar main objective, such as *legato* or *crescendo/decrescendo*. Consequently, I chose one representative example of each style of choral singing discussed in the text: *legato*, leaps, range extension (upward and downward), *crescendo/decrescendo*, and *martellato*. Each choir sings the same exercises so that conductors can compare and contrast the differences in choral tone and technique between ensembles.

I must also explain "good sound." As the adage goes, "Good singing is good singing." A finely trained high school choir performing many styles of literature may be somewhat indistinguishable in tone quality from a college choir (providing an abundance of tenors and second basses!). The key to an outstanding choir rests solely with the conductor's ability to hear in his or her mind's ear a vital, resonant, free, and on-the-breath choral sound. When the singing is right, most other musical factors will be right.

Core Aural Pedagogical Issues

Conductors need to be able not only to teach their choirs how to sing, but they must also be able to hear correct and incorrect vocal technique to continually inform their own teaching. Many conductors I work with have been schooled to listen to problems in pitch and rhythm, and this occupies top priority for such people. Vocal issues are either ignored or placed on a low priority, not by design, but perhaps because of pedagogical habits or lack of instruction.

The skilled conductor must have the ability to prioritize his or her listening depending upon the pedagogical choices he or she establishes prior to the beginning of each rehearsal. It is also my strong feeling that pitch and rhythm training needs to be done separately from training in vocal technique. In fact, if pitch and rhythm are dealt with in the appropriate pedagogical venue, these problems seem to either become minimal or nonexistent.[2] I also believe that issues of choral intonation are twofold. Problems in the ensemble may be vocal problems, aural problems, or a mingling of both. I strongly suggest that vocal issues be dealt with first in the rehearsal and thereby be eliminated from the myriad of problems that could be the cause of sound and pitch issues within the choir.

But, most important, the conductor must train him- or herself to hear vocal technique problems that imbed themselves either throughout the choral ensemble or within one or more voice parts. The core concepts listed on the following page are the focus of this aural tutorial CD.

> I have always believed that there are several essential vocal qualities conductors need to be able to hear immediately within the confines of a choral ensemble rehearsal, regardless of the age of the choir members.

---

2. It has been my experience that the use of choral ensemble solfege has virtually eliminated faulty pitch and rhythm. Ensemble solfege that is harmonically based, such as *Harmonic Immersion Solfege*, provides a tool by which choral singers not only realize a musical score, but by which they determine appropriate intonation. Rhythmic problems, by and large, can be minimized using a metronome to provide a consistent communal tempo through training while learning the piece.

> ## Core Concepts
>
> - Singing on the breath
> - Legato line with *sostenuto*
> - Register consistency
> - Upward leaps sung on the breath
> - Range extension exercises
> - Spacious, high, and forward vocal sound
> - Correct sigh
> - Correct sounds for humming and chewing resonance exercises
> - Chest voice
> - Correct tongue positions for various vowel sounds
> - Closed versus open vowels and their effect upon the choral sound
> - Correct sound of a resonant ensemble hum

Seat the Choir to Maximize Your Ability to Hear and Detect Problems within the Ensemble

In addition to the use of these CDs to build one's ensemble hearing ability, I cannot overemphasize the role of appropriate seating for your choral ensemble. I have written on this subject extensively in Chapter 13 of *The Choral Warm-Up*, but allow me to revisit certain important points presented in that text.

There is no doubt in my mind that such seating arrangements create both pitch and vocal problems for choral singers, and they also make it more difficult for the conductor to hear problems within the ensemble. Block seating arrangements for choirs tend to mask serious vocal issues from the conductor's ears. My major argument against such seating arrangements is that they do not allow for an equal dispersion of choral

> I have long abandoned the traditional way of having each section sit within blocks for both rehearsals and performances.

sound, from the left to the right of the conductor. The sound in block choral seating arrangements tends to travel around the conductor's ear in "chunks" or "blocks." When sound comes to the conductor's ears in such a "coagulated" fashion, it may at times be extremely difficult, in the heat of the rehearsal room, for specific vocal problems to be identified and solved. Problems with choral blend and intonation become hopelessly muddled within such physical arrangements. Also, the singers themselves are hopelessly compromised because they cannot hear well within the ensemble and create vocal problems for themselves because they lose the capacity to monitor their own sound.

It is my recommendation that two adjustments be considered in your choral rehearsal seating to help you hear more accurately in rehearsals: 1) Arrange the singers in rows (see p. 9), with first parts to the conductor's left and second parts to the conductor's right. 2) Shape the arrangement either in a severe semicircle, or in a rectangle surrounding the conductor. This arrangement allows the conductor to be surrounded by sound. Further, this arrangement allows all choral sound to reach the conductor's ears. If a choir sits in a strictly horizontal fashion, some of the ensemble sound will never reach the conductor's ears. In order to improve your hearing ability in rehearsal, you must maximize your ability to hear all the choral sound and also hear various choral details. Block arrangements of choirs tend to blur detail and mask many important attributes that could contribute to a vital and healthy vocal sound.[3]

Further Discussion of the Alto-in-Front Seating Arrangement

Five years ago, I rediscovered the alto-in-front seating arrangement and have never returned to a traditional block arrangement. Weston Noble introduced me to this concept of choral seating. Consider the seating arrangements on the following page for an SATB choir, using a curved formation. The singers marked in boldface are the beginning of the section as determined when an acoustical standing is done.

---

3. I also highly recommend that the conductor experiment acoustically with standing arrangements of his or her choir. The DVD *Achieving Choral Blend through Standing Position* by Weston Noble (GIA DVD-628) outlines how to do this. Many pitch and blend problems can be eliminated using such procedures.

Section One: Introduction and Purpose

T1	T1	T1	T1	T1	**T1**	**T2**	T2	T2	T2	T2	T2
B1	B1	B1	B1	B1	**B1**	**B2**	B2	B2	B2	B2	B2
S1	S1	S1	S1	S1	**S1**	**S2**	S2	S2	S2	S2	S2
A1	A1	A1	A1	A1	**A1**	**A2**	A2	A2	A2	A2	A2

Conductor

or

◀--▶

B1	B1	B1	B1	B1	**B1**	**B2**	B2	B2	B2	B2	B2
T1	T1	T1	T1	T1	**T1**	**T2**	T2	T2	T2	T2	T2
S1	S1	S1	S1	S1	**S1**	**S2**	S2	S2	S2	S2	S2
A1	A1	A1	A1	A1	**A1**	**A2**	A2	A2	A2	A2	A2

Conductor

Regardless of the number of singers in each section, there are four rows *only*. Double rows should not be employed. If one examines this setup, several things become apparent. First, most conductors will agree that it is important for the alto section to be able to hear in order for pitches within the ensemble to remain stable. Placing them in the front row assigns them to the prime hearing and listening location. Second, this setup actually creates a quartet standing arrangement vertically, from front to back. Third, all sections of the choir can hear the bass section because the sound of the bass section comes over the top of the choir. Fourth, choral blend is enhanced because the use of acoustical space is maximized. This arrangement disburses choral sound much more equitably than traditional block arrangements.

Fifth, because of the physical spaciousness of this arrangement, choral sound, or rather the overtones within sections, does not get jammed or backed up. In this arrangement, overtones mix more easily using a spacious acoustic. Sixth, all sections will hear better, especially in polyphonic music. Seventh, the larger voices within your choir will find it easier to sing without tension because they are free to make sound in this arrangement and should not need to lessen their sound or be "shooshed" by the conductor. Eighth, and perhaps most important, this arrangement lessens or eliminates what I refer to as the "choral grunt," which I have experienced when choirs sit sectionally. Because of the abundance of like overtones surrounding them, the vocal mechanism becomes tired and stressed because the environment requires them to make sound.

Also, because of the restricted resonant space around them, they do not accurately perceive their sound and, hence, rely less on the sensation of singing correctly and more on the sound that overcomes them. Those with larger voices tend to become tired, and those with smaller voices tend to push because of the massive amounts of sound around them. Regardless of the acoustic of the rehearsal or performance room, this arrangement is one of the most musically and acoustically efficient arrangements I have used. Choirs that use this arrangement never want to return to more traditional ways of seating. However, for very large symphonic choirs, this arrangement is impractical because of space and stage considerations, and, in the case of large choirs, the striped or vertical sectional arrangements work best.

The Conductor's Ear: How Do We Really Hear?

> What is true for singing and music is also true for language. The left ear is capable of filling in but can never take over that special role which is reserved for the right ear—specifically, the regulator of all phonation, both vocal and linguistic. (p. 25)
>
> —Alfred A. Tomatis
> *The Ear and the Voice*

Use of the Tutorial CDs

The CDs are organized by performing group. Each exercise is presented first in its well-sung version. A period of silence immediately follows each correct example. During this time, you should immediately "replay" (audiate) in your mind's ear what you have just heard without that sound being physically present. Immediately following that silence for audiation is the same exercise containing an imbedded problem.[4]

The conductor must listen repeatedly to each pairing of correct and incorrect versions until he or she is certain of the correct and incorrect sound. The repetition of listening to the recorded "good" example juxtaposed with the exercise with errors is the key to the use of these CDs.

Consistency of Conducting Gestures

The same conductor and accompanist are used on both the college and the high school recordings. This minimizes or possibly eliminates variations in vocal technique that could be caused by inadequate or inconsistent conducting gestures. Conductors should realize that in addition to being able to aurally recognize vocal problems, vocal problems might be caused not by a flawed pedagogical approach to sound, but rather by conducting gestures that are not supportive of choral sound. To minimize these possibilities, conductors are encouraged to consider refreshing their conducting technique through the use of the *Evoking Sound Video: Body Mapping Principles and Basic Conducting Technique* (GIA Publications). To avoid the most frequently observed problems passed from conductors to choir members, which contribute to poor vocal sounds, make sure that: 1) all conducting gestures stay down when the choir sings upward on leaping passages; 2) a subtle or obvious shortening of the core alignment of the body or pressure on the atlanto-occipital joint (forward and down) is not causing a dulling of the choral resonance and a flatting of the pitch; 3) the gesture is released after the ictus, or point of the beat, to encourage good

> Audiation, I believe, is a skill that can be developed through the juxtaposition of sound with silence so that the sound can be recreated in one's hearing without the sound being physically present.

---

4. I am convinced that the ability to hear choral sound in all its dimensions when it is not physically present is at the core of this aural training for conductors. In order for one to evaluate sound in a rehearsal, a model for the parameters of that sound must have been deposited in one's audiation. This skill is fundamental to a conductor's arsenal in the rehearsal room.

breath flow of the choir, and 4) hand position is *not* always parallel to the floor. Poor hand position causes not only the tone to become flat but will encourage back and "jowly" placement of the vowels being sung.

All Conducting Gestures Should Stay "Down" When the Choir Sings Upward on Leaping Passages

In this section, I would like to address, with some specifics, the above-mentioned problems, which I believe cause many of the vocal difficulties within a choral ensemble, regardless of age. My teacher Elaine Brown always said, "There are no bad choirs, only bad conductors." I think she was trying to draw attention to the fact that gesture has a profound and lasting effect upon choral sound. As you begin to develop your aural analysis skills through the use of the enclosed CDs, know that your gestures may be the root cause of your choir's difficulties. The way to correct the problem is to first acknowledge that you might be the cause. Next, experiment with gestures that either eliminate the problem or improve the sound to your ears. While you can improve choral sound with valid and efficient pedagogy, you can almost instantaneously improve the way your choir sings by the way you conduct.

> There are no bad choirs, only bad conductors.
>
> —attributed to Elaine Brown

Hearing Off-the-Breath Singing

> Breath is the liaison between the excitement of feeling
> and the physiological effects. The trained singer especially
> feels this, since he must form the tone on the breath
> as a modulating process—and his success—apart from
> the mastering of the basic technique—is qualitatively
> dependent upon requirements in the area of the soul. (p. 49)
>
> —Meribeth Bunch
> *Dynamics of the Singing Voice*

One of the most fundamental problems at the root of many of the "evils" in choral sound is singing "off the breath." Without a doubt, it is the most often misunderstood concept in workshops I teach. Anyone can understand, in theory, the concept of singing on the breath. However, hearing it and being insistent upon it are different matters! Repeated listening to the on-the-breath and off-the-breath examples on these CDs will hopefully bring pedagogical vigilance and awareness to your rehearsal ears.

To my ear, an on-the-breath sound is unmistakable because of its rich and colorful timbre. Its tone color is both brilliant and tremendously resonant and sonically vibrant.[5] Musical line is constantly moving forward without any impedance when singers are "on the breath."

Sounds that are off the breath are edgy, harsh, loud, thin, and pressed. Often they are accompanied by pitch problems, which are the result, I feel, of a drastic reduction in the number of overtones produced. The thin vocal tone is the result of an unnatural narrowing of the vocal tract because of either an inefficient use of air by the singer or improper use of the body.

Having your body organized like an apple around a core and keeping your gestures down when the choir sings ascending melodic lines will greatly assist the choir in singing on the breath.[6] Again, if one hears the qualities of off-the-breath singing, one needs to counter with experiments concerning repositioning the body and being aware of one's body, in addition to experimenting with the depth of one's beat. Beats that stay "in the bottom of the beat" (an almost tenuto beat) nearly always contribute to and evoke on-the-breath singing by the choir.

> Off-the-breath singing can be unknowingly evoked by conductors when they conduct with an unawareness of their total body and when the gestures do not reflect directly that the singers need to keep the base of support low in the body.

Shortening the Core Alignment of the Body

Aside from encouraging on-the-breath singing at all times, perhaps no problem is more prevalent in conductors and more damaging to choral sound than what Alexander Technique refers to as "the downward and

---

5. In *The Choral Warm-Up*, I spend a great deal of time discussing how to achieve an ensemble sound that is on the breath through the use of physical gestures by the singers. Refer to that publication for further pedagogical information.

6. For conductors who may not understand this concept and want to experience it, the reader is referred to the sections of *The Choral Warm-Up* that discuss on-the-breath singing. The breath-kneading exercise presented will provide the conductor with a way of experiencing both on-the-breath singing and off-the-breath singing.

forward pull." From an anatomical point of view, this results when core body alignment becomes confused in the conductor, and the weight of the body puts pressure upon the atlanto-occipital (A-O) joint, where the top of the spine meets the base of the skull.[7]

Because of one or several intervening alignment malfunctions, the conductor comes off or away from the core points of balance of the body. The result can be seen as a downward and forward pull of the chin. Sometimes this downward, forward pull is minute, and sometimes it is very noticeable. In any case, that pull down will result in an immediate change in the vocalization of the choir. The sound of the choir becomes muffled, less resonant, and less vital and many times begins to flat in pitch. As the choir sings, it is important for the choir to imagine lengthening from the hips to the A-O joint. Freedom of this joint is an absolute necessity for vibrant and free choral sound.

An Inability to "Release" the Gesture after the Ictus

There is a widespread misconception concerning the true nature of the conductor's rebound gesture. The rebound must be a released gesture. That is, after the ictus, or point of the beat, the conductor must be able to let go of the muscles on that rebound so that the arm moves upward in a free and unencumbered fashion. The secret to a free and resonant sound within a choral ensemble rests with the conductor's ability to let go of each rebounded beat. When correctly executed, the rebound of the beat is slower as it moves upward and is not in the tempo of the exercise conducted. The freer the rebound, the more sound will be able to be produced by the choir. If the conductor has any mistrust about the choir's sound, he or she most likely will lock or pull up on the rebound.[8] The result will be a sound that does not move forward and many times is hard, stiff, rigid, flat, and rhythmically sluggish.

---

7. See the Core Points of Balance section of the *Evoking Sound DVD: Body Mapping Principles and Basic Conducting Technique* (GIA DVD-530), which presents valuable Body Mapping principles, and *What Every Musician Needs to Know about the Body* by Barbara Conable, published by Andover Educators and distributed by GIA Publications.

8. See *Evoking Sound* for a further discussion of rebound and its qualities.

A Hand Position Always Parallel to the Floor?

Many approaches to choral conducting advocate using a conducting technique in which the hand is always parallel to the floor. While this may work to some degree when conducting instrumentalists, it has a detrimental effect upon choral tone. From the standpoint of Body Mapping and correct usage, hands used exclusively parallel to the floor inhibit the natural and free movement of the wrist, arms, hands, and scapula. Moreover, when the hand is held parallel to the floor all the time, this encourages the singer to allow the tone to have a back placement. The position of the hand also creates a muffled, dark tone. It is almost impossible to sing with a vibrant and resonant tone when the hands are constantly pointed toward the floor, and it becomes difficult to provide an ictus that affects the choral sound because the ictus is directed toward the floor instead of having its inherent energy directed toward the choir.

The correct position of the hands, at least at the beginning of the pattern, should be similar to the hand position of a handshake. Such a hand position will involve free and efficient movement throughout conducting. A hand held parallel to the floor creates physical tension within the sphere of the conductor's movement and should be avoided.

SECTION TWO
DEVELOPING ANALYTICAL LISTENING SKILLS

Reprioritize Your Listening Skills: How to Develop Pedagogical Listening

Audiation takes place when we assimilate **and comprehend** in our minds music that we have just heard performed or have heard performed sometime in the past. We also audiate when we assimilate **and comprehend** in our minds music that we may or may not have heard but are reading in notation or are composing or improvising. (p. 4)

—Edwin E. Gordon
Learning Sequences in Music: Skill, Content, and Patterns

In Chinese, characters or pictograms communicate ideas and situations. The character for listening attentively consists of the character for Ear, Standing Still, Ten, Eye, Heart, and Mind. According to Zen Master Dae Gak, this pictogram for listening attentively means, "when in stillness one listens with the heart, the ear is worth ten eyes." When we listen for the whole message, our senses need to be poised and focused, like a deer that freezes its gaze in the direction of a lurking predator. (p. 42)

—Rebecca Z. Shafir
The Zen of Listening: Mindful Communication in the Age of Distraction

> Many times, inadvertently, our aural abilities and awarenesses are developed in a very narrow sense, and our training generally does not reflect the profound multidimensionality of the musician's hearing gift.

Many of us who have received musical training are indoctrinated in a certain way regarding listening skills. Generally, those skills are developed along the lines of recognizing and identifying specific issues of only pitch and rhythm.

Aside from pitch and rhythm, musicians can hear tonality (major, minor, dorian, phrygian, etc.), finite timbre differences, color changes, emotional content of tone, and on and on. Yet in our training as conductors, we have not, in general, approached the issues of how to train conductors to hear with depth and pedagogical meaning. For most of us, that training happens on the job, where we ride an intuitive rollercoaster in search of such hearing abilities. Many times, we discover them through equal parts perseverance, accident, and serendipity.

Our ability to hear is in direct relationship, in most cases, to how much rehearsal time we have experienced. On the other hand, I know many conductors who are baffled by such subjects as hearing the "color of the sound," the "resonance of the tone," or the "freedom of the tone." Many other conductors are similarly baffled when I ask them to listen for musical line. For ensembles to sing well, conductors must strive to train themselves to hear as conductors, and, most important, as teachers. I believe that great inroads can be made by practice of this skill outside of the choral rehearsal by learning to re-reprioritize one's hearing sense.

Audiation and Awareness

My teacher Edwin E. Gordon introduced to me one of the concepts that has had the greatest impact upon my conducting and, subsequently, my teaching.[1] Simply stated, audiation is the ability to hear sound without that sound being physically present. In this book, I attempt to develop your audiational skills. The development of listening skills is insufficient if one does not possess the ability to retain sounds in audiation for comparison to other sounds. If one desires the ability to audiate as a conductor needs to, one needs to broaden one's awareness simply by acknowledging, focusing, and reprioritizing the many various dimensions of audiation relevant for conductors.

Key to the acquisition of skills that are most valuable in rehearsal is developing an audiational priority of the factors that both influence and determine vocal production as a first line of analytical hearing. It is also my feeling that audiation can only be developed if one practices audiating!

> Audiation is the ability to hear sound without that sound being physically present.

---

[1]. The concept of audiation, a term Gordon coined, is simplified for purposes of explanation in this tutorial.

Section Two: Developing Analytical Listening Skills

Hence, on these CDs each correct performance of the vocalise contains a silence the exact length of the previous correct musical example. That silence is immediately followed by the incorrect performance of the same vocalise. The work that is done by the conductor during that silent auditional track, I believe, is the key to strengthening his or her "pedagogical ears." In order to make this initial comparison, followed by an inference on new or unfamiliar sounds, correct sound must be retained in audiation to compare that model to the sound with problems.

Please examine the three groups of listening skills below.

Group One Skills: Priority One
- Ability to hear vocal resonances (timbre activity)
- Ability to hear sounds that are high and forward
- Ability to hear sounds that are spacious
- Ability to hear vocalic flow
- Ability to hear on-the-breath singing
- Ability to hear consonants and their correct articulation
- Ability to hear energy in the choral sound through rhythmic clarity
- Ability to hear vowel color
- Ability to hear released and free vocal sounds (relaxed laryngeal positions)

Group Two Skills: Priority Two
- Ability to discriminate pitch
- Ability to discriminate rhythm
- Ability to discriminate between and among musical styles (by color of tone)

Group Three Skills: Priority Three
- Ability to hear human content and spirit in vocal tone

If one examines the list above, many conductors, even young and inexperienced ones, have developed some level of ability in the area of Group Two. Many more experienced conductors can certainly ascertain, to

> Many people believe that one should practice listening. I believe that listening can only improve in relation to one's ability to audiate, that is, hearing choral ensemble sounds when they are not physically present.

some degree, that they have made contributions with characteristics in Group Three. Few conductors have been trained to listen and react to those elements listed in Group One. I have also found that conductors who have some degree of competence in Group One are usually teachers of singing who "double" as choral conductors and have learned and achieved that ability in private voice lessons.

The best place for acquiring finely tuned listening abilities is, indeed, in teaching private studio voice. At the start of my teaching career, after an intensive week of studying how to teach young singers with Helen Kemp, I asked her after class how a clarinetist like me could learn to hear all of those "things."

Her answer is the foundation of this tutorial. She told me three things: 1) Get a few private voice students. THEY will teach you. 2) When you hear a vocal problem that is new, do not necessarily attempt to solve it. When the student is gone, try to make the sound the student made. That imitative process will provide you with an immediate solution. 3) Take voice lessons yourself! That advice was the foundation of my pedagogical approach to developing listening skills. After many years, I believe that this tutorial can help many of you on your way. Although I would encourage you to also pursue Helen Kemp's sage advice to me!

> You may wonder how one can listen to the physical sound of music and audiate at the same time. It is like talking in conversation, where you hear what the other person has said but you do not give it meaning until a very short time after its physical sound is gone and you are actually hearing the next phrase of what is being said. Though it may sound contradictory to what is written in the first paragraph of this handbook, in a word, there is actually only a specious present. We become aware of the present only after it has evaporated in imaginary time. (p. 4)
>
> —Edwin E. Gordon
> *Preparatory Audiation, Audiation, and Music Learning Theory:*
> *A Handbook of a Comprehensive Music Learning Sequence*

Setting Audiational Priorities

One of the shortcomings of training musicians and conductors in particular is that we have not established a hierarchy for practicing and training ourselves to listen. I have found that conductors either listen too broadly and miss fine detail, or they do the opposite and focus on a few minute details at the expense of the larger musical picture. Such listening ability can be compared to viewing an impressionistic painting from a distance. While such a viewing gives one an overall sense of the painting, if that is the only perspective employed, one misses the stunning detail that can only be perceived and appreciated by close observation.

Clearly, what we desire is some middle ground between the two. But that middle ground cannot be achieved, I feel, without some directed and focused study that builds awareness of vocal sounds using audiation as the primary listening tool.

I think it is important to set limits and focus one's study upon the areas needing the most improvement. The Group Two list is familiar to all of us through theory and ear training classes. Group Three requires both experience in rehearsal and out of rehearsal. These skills are acquired through much reading, thought, and inward reflection.

Familiar versus Unfamiliar

The ability to audiate builds another important and often overlooked skill in the development of the conductor's ear. We may learn by rote recognition and comparison of sound, but we learn by inference. That is, we learn new information by our ability to compare information we know immediately to material we do not know. This principle is fundamental for cognitive growth, and it is necessary, I believe, for the growth of the conductor's listening abilities.

One can then select a pedagogical technique to correct the newfound vocal problem. In this process, it is important to categorize and label new problems.[2] This ability to compare and contrast is only possible through careful and patient development of audiational skills specifically geared to

> By making the correctly sung exercises familiar, one will then be able to develop the skill to discern differences in choral ensemble sound and then label the new and unfamiliar sound.

---

2. One's pedagogical language should be consistent. I would recommend using the chapter and topic headings in the vocal technique sections of *The Choral Warm-Up* as departure points.

the vocal needs of the choral conductor. Instrumental conductors, likewise, need to become similarly versed in audiation that is sound specific for instrumental conductors. Perhaps a diagram can help you reprioritize the listening/learning process.

Acquisition of Model Vocal Sounds through Audiational Study by the Conductor

Ensemble sound (present):
↓
Ensemble sound gained through audiational study (past) of model sounds
↓
Comparison of sound in real time with audiationally stored sound
↓
Pedagogical correction of sound
↓
Comparing new ensemble sound to conductor's audiated (learned) model
↓
Further pedagogical refinement
↓
Repeat

> Many conductors believe they are listening to choral sound and the sound of their ensembles when they are, in fact, only passively monitoring that sound.

Monitoring Sound versus an Awareness of Sound

Many conductors only passively monitor the sound of the ensemble. Stated in another way, their listening, instead of being multidimensional and detailed, is usually only taking place on two levels and sometimes three: melodic, rhythmic, and harmonic. Conductors in such a state hear only a wash of sound, almost as if they are standing at a distance and listening to it. I call this sound monitoring, and it usually does not involve audiation. Hence, many details of the music are either vague or very shrouded in the conductor's ear.

Section Two: Developing Analytical Listening Skills

Awareness occurs when sounds are replayed for pedagogical comparison through the use of audiation. Comparisons of correct sounds are subliminally compared through audiation to the actual sounds performed. When one is aware of sound, that state of listening allows one to hear finite details and changes in sound that have to do with vocal production, texture, color, vocalic flow, and musical line.

Understanding and Developing Timbre Acuity: Foreground versus Background

This text attempts to develop one very specific ability in conductors: the ability to discriminate between and among different choral ensemble timbres or textures. I believe that this ability can be developed. However, the starting point for each conductor is a product of nature and nurture.

In any discussion of the multidimensional aspect of music aptitude, the ability to hear timbre in all its dimensions is certainly among the dimensions of the realm of human music aptitude. Like other musical abilities, each person has a certain skill in hearing differences in timbre.[3] The degree of that ability is open for debate.

Edwin E. Gordon, in his *Instrument Timbre Preference Test* (GIA Publications), clearly establishes the existence of timbre preferences in individuals through an objective test. That test assists students nine years of age and older in selecting an appropriate brass or woodwind instrument. Studies show that students who play instruments matching their timbre preferences perform better and have a 50 percent lower dropout rate than students who play instruments not matched to their timbre preference. Since becoming aware of that test, I have been fascinated with the topics of timbre and the conductor's hearing and diagnostic abilities.

Throughout that test, Gordon clearly establishes that each of us has a preference for a specific timbre. As a precursor to this program, it might be helpful for you to take the *Instrument Timbre Preference Test* to determine your timbral preference. This is an important piece of information because when you are focusing on other musical matters such as pitch or rhythm you may only be aware of your timbre preference as a background to pitch and rhythm.

> Awareness of sound is all consuming, while monitoring of sound usually occurs at a safe aural distance from the ensemble.

> One of the objectives of this book is to bring aspects of your hearing that may have heretofore been in the background of your hearing to the foreground.

---

3. Music aptitude has many dimensions: pitch, rhythm, the ability to hear different timbres, and the ability to improvise are among twenty specific areas. We can measure objectively only two of those aptitudes, pitch and rhythm.

I have found that elements that occupy the "background" of our hearing experience usually do not gain our attention and often drift when they are overshadowed by elements in our listening foreground.

From working with conductors, I have learned that they are a product of their musical experiences. For example, conductors whose primary instrument is voice often confine their depth and breadth of timbre recognition to a narrow color spectrum associated very closely with the timbre of the human voice. In many situations, they hear and recognize only the timbres of their own particular voice type. In my experience in teaching organist/conductors, I have found that their "fantasy" about hearing choral colors occupies a much wider spectrum because of their experiences with organ registration. Conductors for whom piano has been their only musical outlet, however, have a narrow timbral and textural sense, which corresponds to what they can produce on the keyboard.

Each of us has a timbre default, which can be identified through the use of Gordon's Timbre Preference Test. Identification of this defect can lead us to an increased state of listening awareness. It then follows that our goal as conductors should be to develop listening sensitivities outside of our timbral preferences.

> It is my belief that each of us has a timbre default. That is, if we do not remain in a state of listening awareness, we will default to our timbre preference.

SECTION THREE
HOW DO YOU HEAR?

How Do We Hear?
Implications of the Thought of Alfred A. Tomatis for Conductors

What is true for singing and music is also true for language. The left ear is capable of filling in but it can never take over that special role which is reserved for the right ear—specifically the regulator of all phonation, both vocal and linguistic (p. 25).

The erect body posture indispensable to finely tuned listening must be accompanied by good posture in the ear itself. What does this mean? Can we really talk about a posture of the ear the same way we do about body posture? Yes, absolutely. Remember that the middle ear has two muscles that use tension to regulate the auditory response curve. It is the inner ear that regulates hearing, and its mechanisms are closely tied to the adaptive responses of the middle ear.

A person whose listening ability is excellent will have good posture. Anyone less adept at listening will have to make an effort to attain it. Achieving the listening posture requires mastering the tension of the muscles of both the stirrup and the hammer, since they form a cybernetic regulatory system that directs the inner ear and adjusts the tension of the eardrum. (p. 86)

—Alfred A. Tomatis
The Ear and the Voice

Once people feel that they have "done enough," they stop stimulating their listening. And their listening reciprocates by not providing them with energy. (p. 147)

The role of these middle ear muscles has been limited to such extreme situations, although recent findings suggest that they are much more important than previously thought. In particular, some audiologists are recognizing that stirrup muscles facilitate sound discrimination. (p. 39)

This new, unorthodox conception of how the ear works follows the model of vision. The first part of the process—the perception of sound—is hearing. The second part—the attuning to sound—is the way of hearing or listening. The middle ear muscles are, therefore, the "listening muscle."

Tomatis remarks that the stirrup muscle is the only one in the body that is in a constant state of tension; it is always working. And because it never rests, we have a chance to rest ourselves. It provides not only protection from external noises, but from internal noises as well.

Listening is the active focusing and protecting function of the ear that permits us to receive what we want and reject what we don't want. (pp. 40–41)

—Paul Madaule
When Listening Comes Alive:
A Guide to Effective Learning and Communication

The thought and work of Alfred Tomatis have great implications for conductors because they provide insight into the interrelationship between the hearing process and the physiology of that process. Because of Tomatis's work, changes in certain physiological and physical factors within the conductor's body can sharpen both the acuity of one's hearing and deepen one's ability to hear subtle changes in texture. Stated in another way, the way you "carry" your body as you rehearse and conduct directly impacts the depth of your listening abilities.

The Functioning of the Ear

The ear has three basic functions. The first is the most obvious, the filtration and analysis of sound by a part of the ear called the cochlea. This function consists of two parts: hearing and listening. Hearing is a passive process, and we have limited abilities to improve this. Listening, however, is the ear's primary function. When the sensations are running smoothly, one can easily process and filter sound. Events such as emotional stress, poor sensory stimulation and communication models, or unpleasant childhood experiences can all encourage a more selective listening process and reduce the desire to listen at all.

The second function is the establishment of spatial dynamic, produced by the vestibular portion of the inner ear. In the inner ear, the vestibule and cochlea are linked to each other and the brain; almost all cranial nerves are somehow connected to the acoustic nerves. Through its strong influence on the fight against gravity and motion detection, the inner ear controls balance, coordination, and muscle tone.

The third (and most debatable) function is the charging or recharging of the brain and, in turn, the body, with electrical potential. A "vibration sensor" within the ear sends this electric message to the brain to give both it and the body energy. When this neuro-charge is combined with the sounds filtered and produced by the cochlea, 90% of the body's total charge can be accounted for by the inner ear. This charge is what sends messages to our joints, bones, and muscles and provides us with the energy to think, create, and move. It is created by high frequency sounds found in Mozart's works and in Gregorian chants. Low frequency sounds that come from rock or rap music make our bodies move to exhaustion, eventually draining energy from the brain.

The inner ear, or vestibular-cochlear system, is one of the first sensory systems to develop in the fetus. By the fifth month, it is fully developed and sending messages to the rest of the nervous system. Early stimulation is vital to the portal central nervous system. This stimulation is caused by high-frequency sounds. Low-frequency sounds, such as heartbeat, breathing, and visceral noises, are filtered out by the amniotic fluid. Therefore, the most dominating sound the developing fetus hears is the high-frequency sound of the mother's voice through bone conduction.

Observations concur with Dr. Tomatis's hypothesis that this voice plays an important role in the developing sensory system of a fetus.

Phonemes are the smallest distinctive units of sound; all languages developed from fifty phonemes. By the seventh month of development, a fetus has a specific, spontaneous muscular response to each phoneme the mother's voice produces. This fascinating sensorimotor response can be inhibited by lack of stimulation or abnormal stimulation, causing the central nervous system to have difficulties perceiving and processing information.

Another possible cause of disorders, learning disabilities, and depression is left ear dominance. Most people are surprised to learn we have a dominant ear, which controls the opposite side of the body (very similar to the brain). People who are right ear dominant have an advantage because the right ear processes much faster. They have more control over the parameter of their voices and speech. According to Tomatis, a study concluded that those with right ear dominance related to situations faster, responded to stimuli more appropriately, and had better control over their emotions. Those with a dominant left ear tended to be more introverted and had less control over their responses to situations. The Tomatis method of auditory training claims to train the right ear to become dominant.

Right Ear Dominance in Vocal Production and Listening: Acquiring More Aural Acuity

Tomatis's work has been applied to the science of vocal production. His theories dwell around the premise that, from a physiological sense, our RIGHT ear is the stronger of our two ears. In fact, the right ear informs the left. Moreover, Tomatis believed that a "listening posture" was and is possible to achieve within one's middle ear! In the world of Tomatis, an adjustment in the body's alignment has a cascading effect upon the muscles that influence the bones of conduction in the middle ear.

The erect body posture indispensable to finely tuned listening must be accompanied by good posture in the ear itself. What does this mean? Can we really talk about a posture of the ear the same way we do about body posture? Yes, absolutely. Remember that the middle ear has two muscles that use tension to regulate the auditory response curve. It is the inner ear that regulates hearing, and its mechanisms are closely tied to the adaptive responses of the middle ear. Depending upon their tension, the muscles of the hammer and stirrup totally modify the auditory response curve. It is as if the desire to listen shapes the curve. (p. 86)

—Alfred A. Tomatis
The Ear and the Voice

We know that the right ear has more connections with the left side of the brain than the left ear. We also now know that the neural link between the left brain and the larynx is shorter. Therefore, ear-to-brain-to-larynx-back-to-ear control loop is more direct for the right ear. That may explain why the right ear is the most efficient zoom for the voice control and other incoming sounds. And, if all goes well, the right ear becomes the leading, listening ear. (p. 44)

—Paul Madaule
*When Listening Comes Alive:
A Guide to Effective Learning and Communication*

Tomatis's research and thought clearly establish that we hear with the right ear. The left ear seems to fill in acoustic and textural detail. If one performs a few simple experiments, this theory seems to be plausible, and it has tremendous import for the refining and focusing of listening abilities of musicians. Interpreting this research for conductors leads to the conclusion that the right ear provides most of the important musical details of our world. Tomatis's research also clearly establishes that we can improve and sharpen our hearing acuity through a combination of alignment awareness and activating.[1]

Establishing a Listening Posture for the Ear

According to Tomatis, one must practice a "listening posture," and that posture can be both practiced and learned. In reading about this listening posture, I realized that in rehearsals and performances, I experience the same sensations that Tomatis describes when maximizing the frequencies of the sound one hears. If one observes conductors in rehearsal and performances, at moments when they are trying to hear in both greater depth and detail, they seem to turn their right ear toward the ensemble! I know that I do this throughout a rehearsal; this turning of the right ear toward the ensemble is instinctive.

If you doubt these theories, think a minute about what you do as a conductor when you want to "listen harder." Many of us, at the most intense part of a rehearsal, will turn either the head or the entire body so as to orient the right side of our bodies, or our right ears toward the ensemble. At those moments, you might also raise your ears a bit, and perhaps lift the forehead. This, according to Tomatis, stretches the muscles of the inner ear, which then affect the amount of sound conducted through the bones of the middle ear. When listening and studying scores, I believe you can increase the depth of listening by maintaining what Tomatis calls a "listening posture." Once this aligned listening posture is established, you will hear with more depth.

I have found that if I maintain a listening posture while I study a score through listening or in a rehearsal my ability to hear grows exponentially. I strongly suggest that one employ this "listening posture" whenever engaged with music.

---

1. I highly recommend Paul Madaule's book *When Listening Comes Alive: A Guide to Effective Learning and Communication*. In that book, the author gives a series of "earobics" exercises to heighten aural acuity.

SECTION FOUR
IDENTIFYING ASPECTS
OF TIMBRE

What Is Choral Timbre?

Choral timbre, as well as any timbre that is the result of human interactions in a music situation, is the result of many factors. (I use the terms "timbre" and "texture" interchangeably.) Choral sounds may be as wide or as narrow as your ability to hear and fantasize about timbre. A major gift for any conductor is his or her ability to fantasize about the texture (timbre) of the sound. For choral musicians, the carrier of choral color (timbre) is the resonance and/or shape of the vowel. Within each vowel is a world of color, resonance, and intensity that is often referred to as texture. Different languages, via vowel sounds, are the carrying vehicles for an entire world of color within a choral ensemble tapestry. The vowel carries the color of that language, and consonants contribute to the nature of the rhythm and expression.

The conductor should develop listening skills for vowel timbres first. In fact, I have found that when many conductors listen to a choral sound, they do not hear the texture of each vowel sound. They hear, instead, a foreground of pitch and rhythm and a background of very vague and somewhat "white" or rather nondescript "sound." The ability to simply recognize the bolder areas of choral timbre is insufficient for our needs. The ability to hear the depth of the timbre is one way of thinking about the subject.

This is the first step in moving beyond one's natural timbre defaults. That is, each of us will default to a predetermined list of things to listen to in a choral sound based upon our experiences and biases. I believe you can teach yourself to hear other textures, timbres, and colors outside the parameters or defaults determined by your own experiences, but to do that takes a certain amount of study and awareness of other possibilities in the aural textural world. It is my hope that this book and the recording of the Core Vocal Exercises will start you on that process.

> Another way to hear the depth of the timbre is to consider the ability to fantasize about vowel resonance, initially, as either "tall/narrow" or "round."

Be Aware of Your Timbre Defaults

The point I am trying to establish is that each of us has timbre preferences or timbre defaults. That is, when we listen with a certain degree of unawareness, we may only be vaguely aware of timbres that lie outside the realm of our personal preferences! Personal timbral preferences (or biases) are strong within musicians.

The task, it then seems to me, is to expand one's textural palette. Timbre defaults can be extremely dangerous. If one does not become aware of timbres other than his or her own preferences, it will be impossible for the ensemble to vary timbre as style, human, and textual demands require. In expanding your listening skills, the job is to begin to hear timbres outside your defaults. Then, and only then, will your choir realize a brilliant and flexible spectrum of choral sound.

There is another aspect to all of this to consider. If one can hear or fantasize about choral timbre, that ability transfers directly into the sound of the choral ensemble. The reasons are many. What one hears will transfer to the ensemble through gestural suggestion. The choir will only reflect what you hear, regardless of the timbre of their voices or their abilities.

Your ear and the depth of your hearing awareness can directly influence the sound of the ensemble. There is truth to the statement that you conduct with your ear!

Aural Models Acquired Outside This Tutor

Aside from the foundational material presented in this tutor, once one's hearing and listening skills have been readjusted to focus on matters of vocal production through the development of audiational skills, one can acquire additional vocal models from a variety of other resources, mainly commercial recordings of exemplary choirs. Repeated listening and study of such recordings can educate and inform biases regarding vocal tone and production, and that newfound information can be brought to bear on sounds during rehearsals. The final section of this volume contains a recommended list of recordings selected on the basis of vocal sound and musical line. Analysis of these recordings can further aurally inform the pedagogical directions you take with your choir in the rehearsal room.

> The choir will only reflect what you, the conductor, are aware of.

Posttest Evaluation

At the end of the tutorial section of the CD is a practice test. At the conclusion of the aural study of these exercises, the conductor should listen to the posttest portion and answer the questions contained in the section of this book titled Progress Test Question Sheet. Answers for this test are given on page 115 of this book. The conductor should review any exercises he or she missed on the posttest and then retake the entire progress test.

The Role of the Accompanist

One of the byproducts of this tutorial CD, especially on the tracks that are correctly sung, is being able to determine the keyboard factors that support good, healthy, free singing. At the beginning of the CD, there are several tracks devoted to simple instructions to accompanists read by Marilyn Shenenberger, the arranger of the accompaniments for these exercises. All the exercises used on these CDs are contained in *The Choral Warm-Up: Core Vocal Exercises* (GIA, G-6397). Categories that the conductor should listen for are:

- Piano technique involved when the choir ascends
- Keyboard voicing of the exercises
- Voicing of the dominant function notes placed within the exercises to assist with intonation
- Piano pedaling indications
- Sound and timbre of the piano as it relates to the vocal technique used by the choir
- Direction of musical line
- Inner phrasing of accompaniments

Essentials of Vocal Listening for the Conductor: Root Problems

There are a few basic principles Frauke Haasemann and Helen Kemp taught me to follow when listening for vocally correct sounds. One recommended approach is to listen to all the correct exercises and only listen for a single factor. Many times, conductors hopelessly confuse and confound their ears by trying to listen to too many vocal problems at once. Most choral ensemble vocal problems have a root vocal problem, which then causes a chain reaction of other vocal and intonation problems. If one can find the root vocal problem, many of the other difficulties disappear. Those root problems are: 1) on-the-breath singing, 2) unspacious, pressured singing, and 3) sounds that are not high and forward enough. I will address each briefly, but before I do that, let me briefly mention the issues of recognizing pitch and rhythm errors when they appear.

Hearing Pitch and Rhythm: Score Preparation Is the Key

One should not devote valuable rehearsal time to hunting out pitch and rhythm problems. A conductor's work concerning pitch and rhythm error detection must be done before the rehearsal process as part of any score preparation process. When preparing a score, the conductor should sing and learn each vocal part separately. As a second step in this process, the conductor should then sing one part and play another.

Only when all possible singing and playing permutations have been accomplished should one feel confident moving to rehearsal. If one adheres to this tedious and meticulous process, pitch and rhythm errors will become a spontaneous, almost intuitive, process, thereby leaving valuable rehearsal and listening time for detecting vocal issues within the sound of the ensemble. With methodical score study, the detection of pitch and rhythm problems becomes as effortless as the naming of the predominant colors in a picture. Rhythm and pitch error detection should not be the primary awareness of the conductor. Issues of timbre must have the highest listening priority in the conductor's listening hierarchy. Conductors who continually harass a choir concerning pitch issues are usually unaware of more serious vocal difficulties that may be contributing to or causing the symptom.

> The energy needed for active and aware listening and analysis must be reserved in the rehearsal for the hearing and diagnosis of vocal problems.

On-the-Breath Singing

Of all the questions I have been asked in workshops, this is the most frequently asked: "What does it sound like when a choir is off the breath?" When a choir sings off the breath, two dangerous pedagogical problems rear their ugly heads. Because the breath is not taken properly or portioned correctly, this lack of adequate, pressurized airflow causes the larynx to rise. The aural evidence of this is a hard, edgy, loud sound, a sound that has inherent tension as evidenced by a lack of rich vocal color. Loud is the operative word here.

On the opposite end of the spectrum, I have heard many high school choral directors, who in their attempt to avoid such a hard sound, retreat in the opposite vocal direction to a lighter sound palette that "tunes" easily. This is just as dangerous and is another type of off-the-breath singing. This type of vocalism causes insufficient airflow that does not allow the vocal folds to completely close. Dynamic ranges in such a sound are narrow, and the choir cannot usually sing in tune for any period of time. On-the-breath singing is characterized by a free, vibrant, and rich tone that also sounds full. On-the-breath singing is also characterized by sound (or musical line) that moves freely forward, propelled by appropriate movement of air by the singer.

Unspacious, High Larynx Singing

As I stated above, unspacious, high larynx singing often goes hand in hand with off-the-breath singing. When a high larynx is present, one will immediately hear a drastic reduction in both the resonance and overtones in the sound. Upper register notes or approaches to upper register singing become difficult, if not impossible, to execute. Choral sounds seem pressurized or pressed. In some instances there is also either a flatting or sharping of the sound. Both problems must be addressed before the choral ensemble can make any significant progress toward healthy, free, and resonant choral sound. Sounds produced from a high, tensed laryngeal position will also suffer at times from a lack of high and forward vocal placement.

Sounds that Are Not High and Forward

There is a resonant brilliance and clarity of pitch core when choral ensemble sounds are high and forward. Sounds that lack high, forward placement are dull in color, almost foggy. In such sounds, you are unable to ascertain the exact core of the pitch. In fact, most intonation problems in choral ensembles are created by a lack of sufficiently high and forward placement. Much of the problem with high and forward sounds has to do with having an English-speaking choir.

The major objective in working with American choirs is to be vigilant about the high and forward placement of every sung sound. Jowly vowels lack brilliant resonance and consequently manifest themselves in flat or dull pitch.

Help for Hearing Subtleties of Vocal Sound: Color

Many experienced and inexperienced conductors, when asked to listen to dimensions of vocal sound other than pitch and rhythm, become baffled and confused. Some claim that all they hear are pitches and rhythms. Others claim they can't hear much of anything.

As mentioned before, vocalists who do not play another instrument tend to hear in narrow color palettes. That, perhaps, is the root of the problem. The first ten years of my musical life were spent as a wind player, and the colors that surrounded me as a wind band instrumentalist, I am certain, stimulated my sense of color and texture and most certainly expanded my hearing spectrum. In the early twentieth century, William Finn wrote extensively in his volumes entitled *The Art of the Choral Conductor* on the choral conductor's need to hear vocal sounds as instrumental timbres. Finn heard voices as reeds or brass, oboes or flutes, etc. According to Finn, one's ability to hear vocal sounds as instrumental timbres contributes to an expanded palette of choral sound.

Hearing vowel colors is essential to diagnostic ensemble listening. Without the ability to hear different colors, one will most certainly miss subtle changes in each sound. Several years ago, I heard Marilyn Horne teach a master class to a young mezzo-soprano. Miss Horne asked the young singer what colors she was singing. The singer looked stunned and had no answer. Miss Horne replied, "Dear, you should always sing colors. Sing this Brahms song in the most luxurious purple velvet you can envision." Needless to say, the difference in the singer's tone was astounding.

I often ask conductors to assign specific colors to what they want to hear. In fact, I have not been above asking conductors to pick specific colors from one of those boxes of 100 Crayola crayons. Later in this text, I address this procedure more fully. The change in both their conducting and the ensemble's sound is always remarkable.

> American English has many dialectic variants, but, as a rule, American English suffers from a backward or jowly placement.

> The doorway to detailed listening skills is to develop a sense of fantasy about sound and, thus, a vastly expanded awareness concerning the details within each choral sound.

Section Four: Identifying Aspects of Timbre

To my ear, changes in the vocal technique of the choir radically change the color of the choral sound to my ears. Sound that is off the breath sounds gray to me. Round, resonant vowels tend toward the scarlet/burgundy end of the spectrum; some pressed sounds are metallic silver to my ears. However, I can say that whatever the sound, a color is always vivid in my fantasy at the moment, and that color occupies the *highest* priority in my listening. So I believe it might be helpful for you to begin hearing in color! Associate both good sounds and bad sounds with particular colors. The fantasy of such colors will also serve the dual purpose of clearly organizing specific sounds in your audiation for recall and comparison. In the workbook section of this tutor, I attempt to guide you to make such choices.

Omnipresent Necessity for Musical Line: Hearing Musical Line

In consideration of the facets of phrasing it is helpful, it seems to me, to think of melody as musical energy. The child's definition is not utter nonsense; "melody is a note looking for a place to sit down." Melody, as an abstraction, lies in the quality of tension or relaxation passed by each note to its successor (or received from its predecessor) until the musical sentence is complete and the moment of rest occurs.

Abstractions are seldom without a set of contradictory data, but I have found it helpful to theorize that there are but three "postures" (or conditions of melodic "energy": 1) "Departing from…" 2) "Passing through…" and 3) "Arriving at…" (pp. 79–80)

—Robert Shaw
The Robert Shaw Reader

Listening for Issues of Rhythmic Energy and Clarity

To my way of thinking, there is a prerequisite that should be contained in every sound heard by the conductor and produced by the ensemble: rhythmic energy. While this quality may be difficult to describe, it is not difficult to hear.

For a sound to be considered even borderline healthy, it must contain a certain amount of energy that propels vowels forward in time. That energy is supplied by the spirit and commitment of the singers and also the amount of connection and awareness they have concerning both the sound and themselves. Those energies are carried on the breath stream. Energy content is a prerequisite in all sounds that submit themselves to the conductor's evaluation and diagnosis. No other vocal issues should be dealt with until there is a sufficient amount of energy in the musical line. On these tutorial CDs, energy content was not an issue, but the energy within the sound of your ensemble may be.

Please be aware that the root of many choral ensembles' tone problems rests in a basic energy that is not supplied by the choir. This should be addressed before trying to solve any vocal problems.

What does a lack of rhythm sound like? The sound is sluggish, and the musical line seems to plod along. In these sounds, musical lines do not assume any shape, and there is an overall boredom. When listening to your choir, especially on vocalises, make certain that there is an almost effervescent energy.[1]

> Rhythmically vital sound has both an excitement and a resonance that is unmistakable.

Aggressiveness in Sound

A caution: The solution to the problem of a lack of rhythmic energy is not for the conductor to simply supply more energy through gesture or body language. Such an approach usually can be characterized by a hyper conducting style, and a "throwing" of rhythm at the choir through a tight and controlled gesture. This aggressiveness is oftentimes the product of insecurities on the part of the conductor or suggests a total inability to hear any aspects of choral texture except pitch and rhythm. Such an approach

---

1. For specific suggestions on energizing choral sound, the reader is referred to *The Choral Warm-Up*, pp. 134–138.

usually results in what I refer to as an aggressive choral sound, which is usually hard, edgy and loud and generally stays the same color no matter the style or composer. This sound is almost always accompanied by a tight, muscular gesture from the conductor, who is trying to "make" the ensemble sing. Yes, the sound must be rhythmic, but that responsibility is the singers' and the singers' alone. Rhythmic energy supplied externally by the conductor always affects the choral sound detrimentally.

Moreover, I have found that conductors who engage in this activity never really hear the sound of their choir because of the amount of energy they are pushing onto the ensemble and into their sound. Energy used to throw rhythm at the choir is energy taken away or subtracted from one's ability to hear. Please step back, listen, and make sure this is not a characteristic of your choir![2]

> Conductors who aggressively pursue rhythmic drive through gesture hopelessly compound not only the vocal problems of singers but stifle musicianship.

---

2. I fully realize that I have opened up a very difficult question for many here. The solution is not easy, and many of the issues that pertain to aggressive choral sounds deal with the mimetics of the conductor. This concept of mimetics is discussed at length in my book *The Musician's Soul* and revisited in *The Musician's Spirit* and *The Musician's Walk*.

SECTION FIVE
THE CONDUCTOR'S AURAL WORKBOOK

Section Five: The Conductor's Aural Workbook

Introduction

Marilyn Shenenberger narrates the first twenty-eight tracks of both CDs, which are accompanist suggestions.[1] In our workshops in the two years since these exercises were written, there have been many questions regarding the playing of these exercises. Marilyn is a master at accompanying these vocalises in such a way that the vocal sound of the choir is always supported. From the start of the rehearsal, she trains the choir's listening ears through what she does and does not play at the keyboard. While one can certainly ascertain what she is doing by listening to the recorded examples, we have found it helpful for accompanists to understand the most important technical information about the playing of each exercise. Shenenberger gives a few points of advice concerning the playing of the exercises. The tracks and their specific content are listed starting on the following page.

---

1. All twenty-four exercises presented in *The Choral Warm-Up* are included on the CD by Shenenberger that accompanies that textbook. The CD is also available in the Accompanist Supplement edition.

Accompanist Suggestions: Marilyn Shenenberger

Track Description

1. Introduction: Marilyn Shenenberger
2. Performing modulations: Marilyn Shenenberger—Short performing specifics for each of the Core Vocal Exercises performed on this CD with the choirs. Please note that incorrect performances also have incorrectly played accompaniments.
3. Accompanist performing specifics: Exercise 1 explanation

Exercise 1

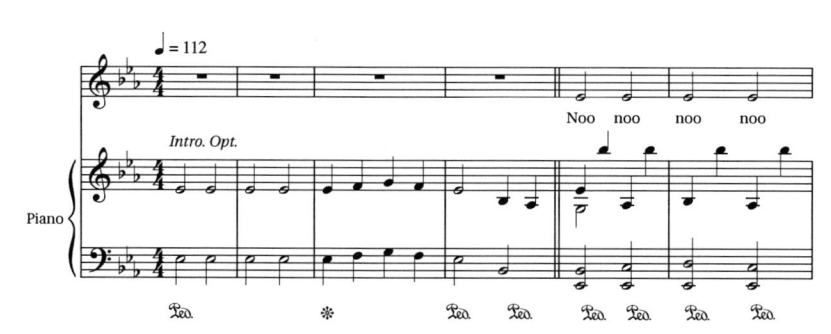

Track Description

4. Accompanist performing specifics: Exercise 1 accompaniment
5. Accompanist performing specifics: Exercise 2 explanation

Exercise 2

Section Five: The Conductor's Aural Workbook

Track Description

6 Accompanist performing specifics: Exercise 2 accompaniment

7 Accompanist performing specifics: Exercise 3 explanation

Exercise 3

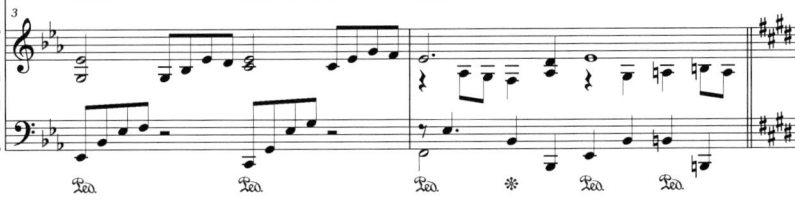

Track Description

8 Accompanist performing specifics: Exercise 3 accompaniment

9 Accompanist performing specifics: Exercise 5 explanation

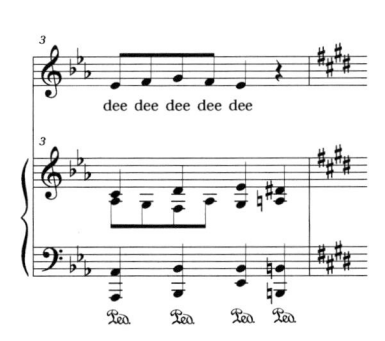

Exercise 5

Track Description

10 Accompanist performing specifics: Exercise 5 accompaniment

11 Accompanist performing specifics: Exercise 6 explanation

Exercise 6

Track Description

12 Accompanist performing specifics: Exercise 6 accompaniment

13 Accompanist performing specifics: Exercise 8 explanation

Exercise 8

Section Five: The Conductor's Aural Workbook

Track Description

14   Accompanist performing specifics: Exercise 8 accompaniment

15   Accompanist performing specifics: Exercise 9 explanation

Exercise 9

Track Description

16   Accompanist performing specifics: Exercise 9 accompaniment

17   Accompanist performing specifics: Exercise 13 explanation

Exercise 13

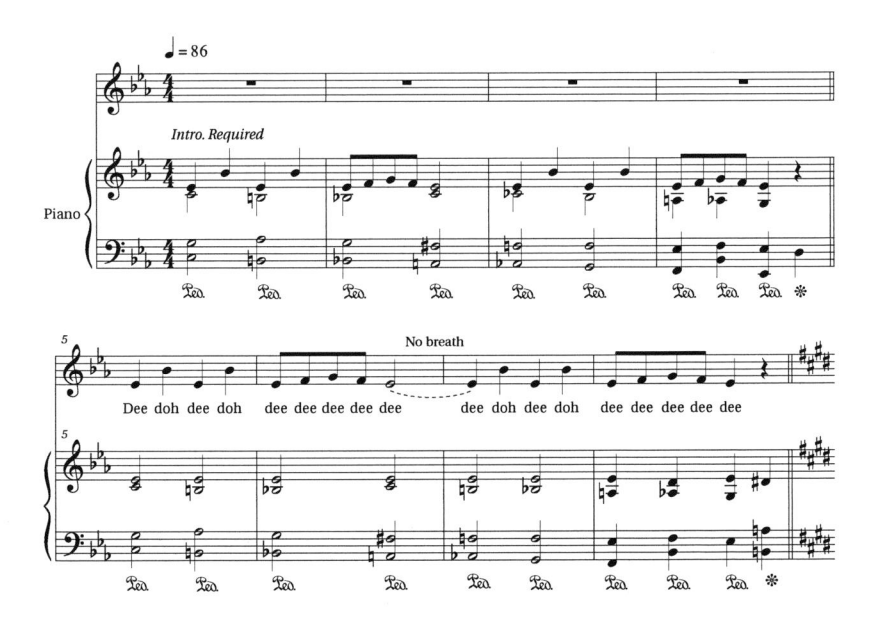

The Choral Conductor's Aural Tutor • James Jordan

Track Description

18 Accompanist performing specifics: Exercise 13 accompaniment
19 Accompanist performing specifics: Exercise 14 explanation

Exercise 14

Dee dee dee dee dee   dee dee dee dee dee   Doh

Track Description

20 Accompanist performing specifics: Exercise 14 accompaniment
21 Accompanist performing specifics: Exercise 17 explanation

Exercise 17

Nee__ noh__ nee__

Track Description

22 Accompanist performing specifics: Exercise 17 accompaniment
23 Accompanist performing specifics: Exercise 18 explanation

Exercise 18

Dee__ dee__

Section Five: The Conductor's Aural Workbook

Exercise 18, cont.

Track Description

24 Accompanist performing specifics: Exercise 18 accompaniment

25 Accompanist performing specifics: Exercise 19 explanation

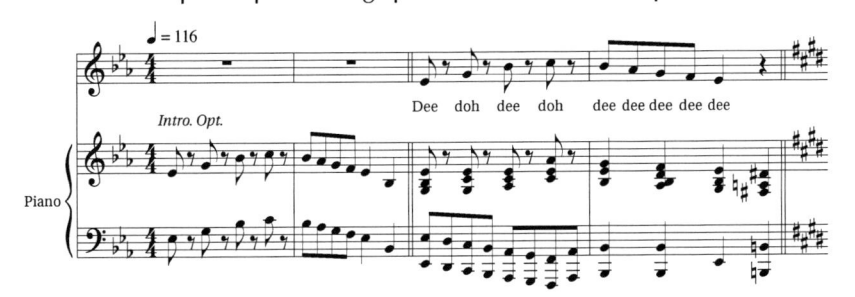

Exercise 19

Track Description

26 Accompanist performing specifics: Exercise 19 accompaniment

27 Accompanist performing specifics: Exercise 24 explanation

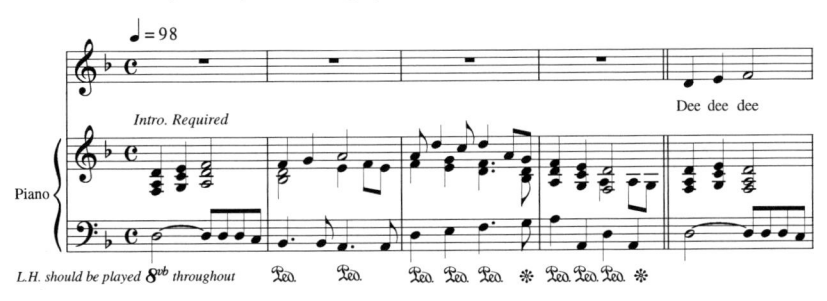

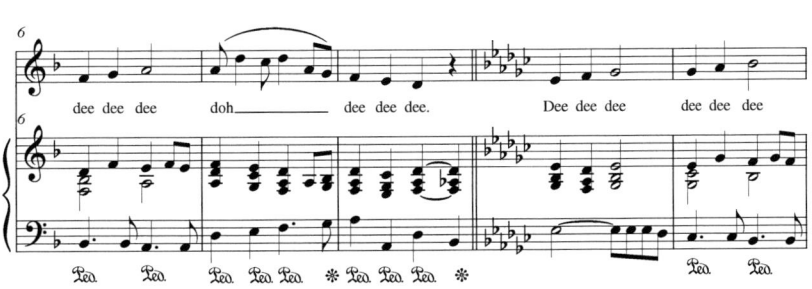

Exercise 24

Track Description

28 Accompanist performing specifics: Exercise 24 accompaniment

As an aside, I must say that not only the musical composition of these exercises but the decisions Marilyn has made in order to support the sound of the choir have made a profound impact upon the sound of the ensembles we teach and I conduct. I am certain that these exercises played well, combined with your newfound diagnostic hearing sense, will greatly improve your teaching and support your conducting.

Core Vocal Exercises: Model Exercises and Embedded Problems

For a majority of the exercises presented on the CDs, the choir performs a correct version followed by a silence the exact length of that exercise. In that space, the listener should try to audiate the example that was just performed. That is, one should be able to hear the exercise previously sung without the sound being physically present. In doing this, one builds a strong diagnostic hearing sense by developing the ability to recall the performed exercise without the sound being physically present. The ability to both retain in audiation and recall what one has heard is fundamental to the listening that will inform wise and prudent pedagogical descriptions.

For each incorrectly performed exercise below, a short description of the problem is discussed. A cross reference is also included for *The Choral Warm-Up* text for further study and clarification of both the problem and its pedagogical solution, if desired. This cross-referencing is always indicated with the icon: .

Central to a conductor's acute hearing ability is the ability not only to recognize that a problem exists but to accurately delineate the overall problem into specific subparts. Many conductors have the ability to determine that something isn't right but are unable to describe specific problems within the sound. This is especially true with new teachers and conductors. What makes the process even a bit more difficult is that several problems may embed themselves in a single sound. It is important to be able to hear composite sounds with multifaceted issues! In order to be able to develop such skills, one must be able to accurately describe the quality or qualities of sound one is hearing.

The only way to develop this ability is to write short, accurate descriptions of each problem that are meaningful to you. During my

> Most important, perhaps, to this entire process is your ability to verbally describe in exacting terms the vocal problem you hear.

studies with Edwin E. Gordon, he always said that if you can't write something accurately, you probably would not be able to teach it effectively. Time and experience have taught me the wisdom of that advice. Hence, these materials are designed to force you to verbalize and, yes, objectively describe a problem in concrete, descriptive language. The clearer the expression of the problem, the more apparent the pedagogical solution will be. Consequently, the most important aspect of this workbook section is the required journaling after each exercise with the embedded problem. It may take you several listenings to accurately describe what you hear, but describe you must. Do not be content to merely identify and label a problem. In order to craft a pedagogical solution, you must accurately describe the problem so that you can both remember the problem when it appears again and use that same language in crafting a solution.

Issues of Register Breaks: A Problem that Masks Other Problems

Another cautionary note: One of the problems that should be eliminated from the outset is the one concerning register breaks particular to each voice part. My experience is that music that hovers around the voice break creates vocal havoc in its own right. In fact, music that hovers on a vocal break may sound like another problem. So it is my suggestion that before you apply the aural skills learned in this book to your literature, you visually analyze each voice part to determine that it does not hang inordinately long on such breaks. Solutions for solidifying vocal sound through register breaks are many, but there is general agreement that support should be maintained when going through a break and that a brighter sound should be maintained. At times, depending upon the voice part, closing the vowel may minimize the problem. The areas of concern should be: female voices in the area of B in the treble clef and F at the top of the treble clef, for tenors around F at top of tenor clef, for baritones at middle C, and for bass-baritones from G to A-flat at the top of the bass clef.[2]

---

2. A detailed examination of register breaks can be found in Howard Swan's chapter concerning the history of choral sound in America in *Choral Conducting Symposium* edited by Harold A. Decker and Julius Herford. In that writing, the section devoted to the Westminster School of Choral Sound contains the detailed discussion of lifts in each particular voice according to the teachings of John Finley Williamson.

Accuracy of Language When Analyzing Aural Examples

Use language that is not colloquial or slang to describe the problems you hear. Search for language pertaining to the qualities of vocal sound that is concise, clear, and accurate. Describing sound as "mushy," "ugly," or "scary" will not lead you to accurate pedagogical solutions. Also, if you use that language with yourself, I can guarantee you that you will use it when you are teaching. Such vague language hopelessly confuses amateur singers, and one should avoid such verbalism at all costs. To help you begin your pedagogical vocabulary, allow me to begin a list of terms and phrases that you might possibly use:

- Edgy
- Disembodied
- Unspacious
- White
- Resonant
- Rigid
- Glass-like
- Locked
- Backward
- Tall and narrow
- Having a pitch core
- Open
- Covered
- Free
- Pointed
- High
- Sluggish
- Centered
- Colorful
- Elastic
- Buoyant
- Warm
- Focused
- Having rhythmic breathing
- Sung with stroke

- Bright
- Pressed
- Bland
- Rich
- Hard
- Tight
- Metallic
- Jowly
- Forward
- Round
- Having a core to the sound
- Closed
- Spinning
- Vibrant
- Breathy
- Tense
- Vital
- Ringing
- Flexible
- Supple
- Round
- Clear
- Colorful
- Sounding as though the choir sings through the rest

- Bowed (lots of string images)
- Using images: banana space (vs. sandwich pace), fly fishing, basketball head (with nose at point where lines converge) for round sound
- Vertical (space)
- Directed
- Sounding like it is poured
- Generous
- Open
- Ethereal
- Weepy
- Noble (posture)
- Pointed
- Domed
- With continual motion through long notes and the phrase as a whole
- Connected
- Spun
- Horizontal (line)
- Having an egg space (especially in French, in front of mouth)
- Natural
- Emotional
- Joyful
- Pure
- Personal

Other "negative" terms:
- Tight
- White
- Static
- Poked
- Pushed or forced
- Throaty
- Fluttery (can also be positive)
- Pressed
- Thin
- Punched
- Manufactured
- Wide or spread
- Generic

The Tutorial Exercises: Instructions

1. Listen to the correct version of each vocalise. In the silent space after the exercise, immediately attempt to audiate the exercise exactly as you heard it. Repeat the track with the correct performance of the exercise as many times as necessary to accurately audiate the exercise when the sound is not physically present. Your ability to diagnose problems within the ensemble is only as good as your ability to audiate a correct sound. That audiated sound is the standard by which you will compare problem exercises and arrive at effective pedagogical descriptions.

2. After listening to the exercise with a problem, immediately write descriptive terms in the space provided. You must write something. These descriptive terms will be the way you will remember incorrect sounds in your audiation when you are actually in front of your choir.
3. If you cannot write something to describe the incorrect sound, chances are high that you have not retained in your audiation the sound of the correct exercise. If this happens, return to listening to the correct exercise until you can retain it, long-term, in your audiation.

Section Five: The Conductor's Aural Workbook

CD 1: The Westminster Williamson Voices

Accompanist Suggestions: Marilyn Shenenberger

Track	Description
1	Introduction: Marilyn Shenenberger
2	Performing modulations: Marilyn Shenenberger—Short performing specifics for each of the Core Vocal Exercises performed on this CD with the choirs. Please note that incorrect performances also have incorrectly played accompaniments.
3	Accompanist performing specifics: Exercise 1 explanation
4	Accompanist performing specifics: Exercise 1 accompaniment
5	Accompanist performing specifics: Exercise 2 explanation
6	Accompanist performing specifics: Exercise 2 accompaniment
7	Accompanist performing specifics: Exercise 3 explanation
8	Accompanist performing specifics: Exercise 3 accompaniment
9	Accompanist performing specifics: Exercise 5 explanation
10	Accompanist performing specifics: Exercise 5 accompaniment
11	Accompanist performing specifics: Exercise 6 explanation
12	Accompanist performing specifics: Exercise 6 accompaniment
13	Accompanist performing specifics: Exercise 8 explanation
14	Accompanist performing specifics: Exercise 8 accompaniment
15	Accompanist performing specifics: Exercise 9 explanation
16	Accompanist performing specifics: Exercise 9 accompaniment
17	Accompanist performing specifics: Exercise 13 explanation
18	Accompanist performing specifics: Exercise 13 accompaniment
19	Accompanist performing specifics: Exercise 14 explanation
20	Accompanist performing specifics: Exercise 14 accompaniment
21	Accompanist performing specifics: Exercise 17 explanation
22	Accompanist performing specifics: Exercise 17 accompaniment
23	Accompanist performing specifics: Exercise 18 explanation
24	Accompanist performing specifics: Exercise 18 accompaniment
25	Accompanist performing specifics: Exercise 19 explanation
26	Accompanist performing specifics: Exercise 19 accompaniment
27	Accompanist performing specifics: Exercise 24 explanation
28	Accompanist performing specifics: Exercise 24 accompaniment
29	Comments on incorrect tracks and accompaniment on incorrect tracks

The Choral Conductor's Aural Tutor • James Jordan

Exercises and Notebook for The Westminster Williamson Voices

TRACK 30　　　　Exercise 1, Legato; Line (Correct)

Color of sound and/or descriptions for correct sound:

TRACK 31　　　　Exercise 1, Legato; Line (Incorrect)
　　　　　　　　Problem = women sing with little head tone in the sound

p. 76

Descriptors for vocal problems:

Section Five: The Conductor's Aural Workbook

TRACK 32   Exercise 2, Repeated Tone with *Crescendo* and *Decrescendo* (Correct)

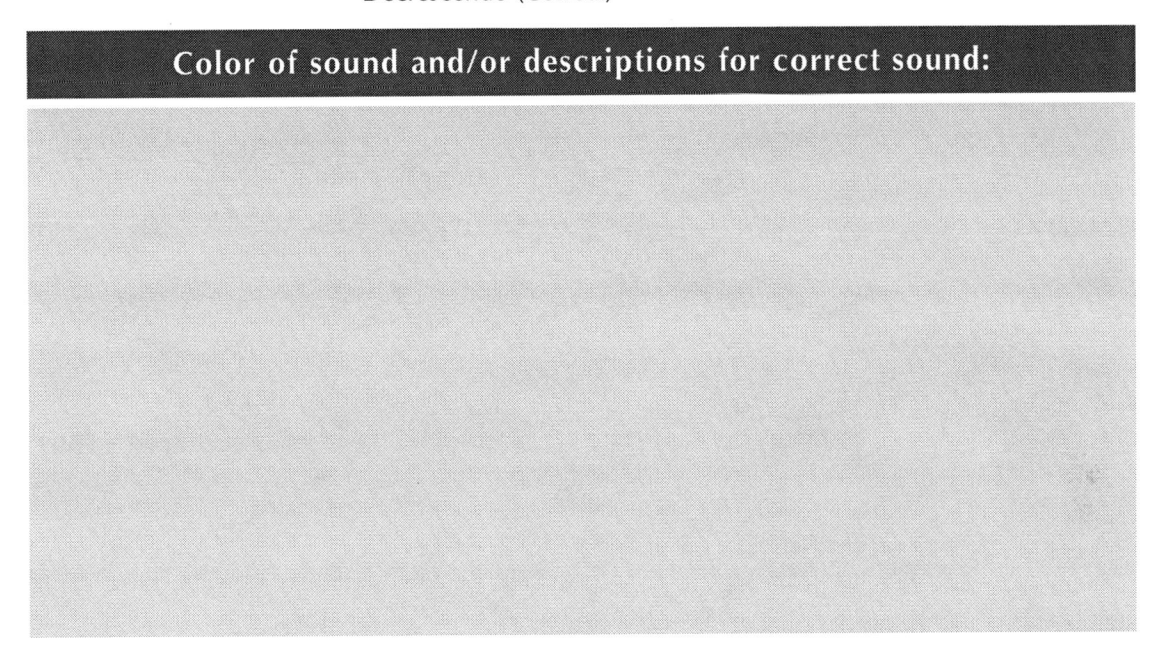

Color of sound and/or descriptions for correct sound:

TRACK 33   Exercise 2, Repeated Tone with *Crescendo* and *Decrescendo* (Incorrect)

pp. 94–95, 136   Problem = sluggish movement to vowel

Descriptors for vocal problems:

The Choral Conductor's Aural Tutor • James Jordan

TRACK 34 Exercise 5, Singing on Breath through Moving
Eighth Notes (Correct)

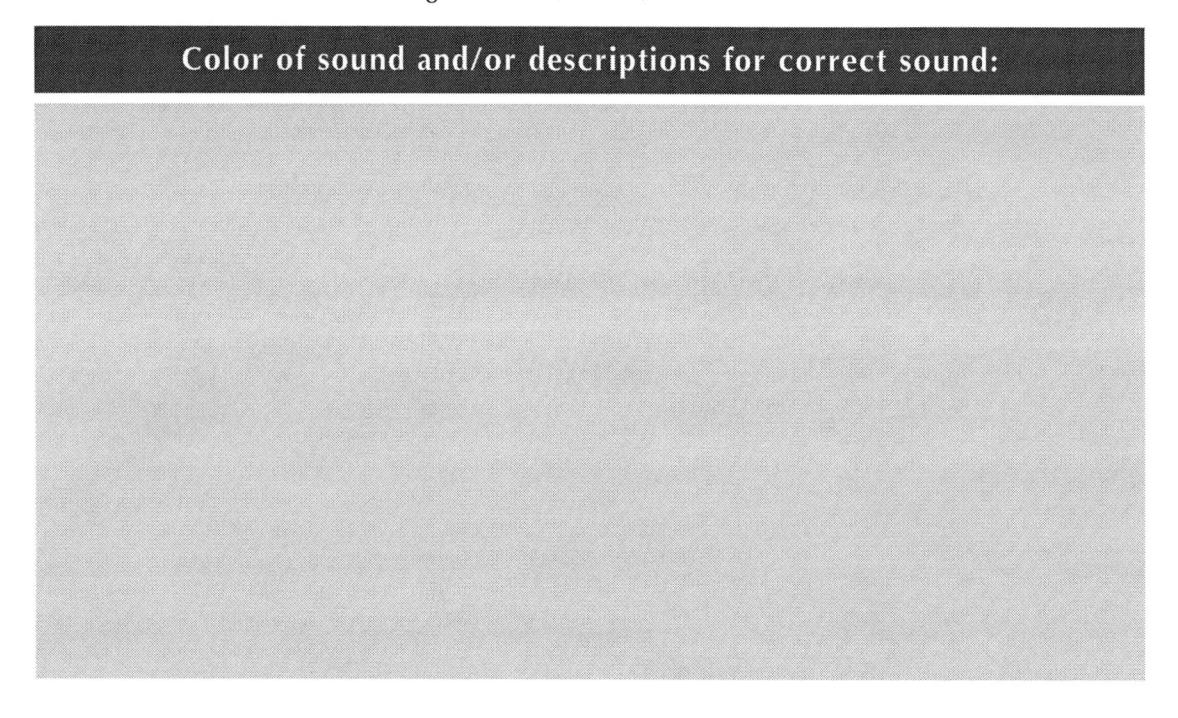

Color of sound and/or descriptions for correct sound:

TRACK 35 Exercise 5, Singing on Breath through Moving
Eighth Notes (Incorrect)

pp. 83, 108–109 Problem = tongue position for "ee" vowel is not high enough

Descriptors for vocal problems:

Section Five: The Conductor's Aural Workbook

TRACK 36   Exercise 6, Register Consistency with Downward Leaps (Correct)

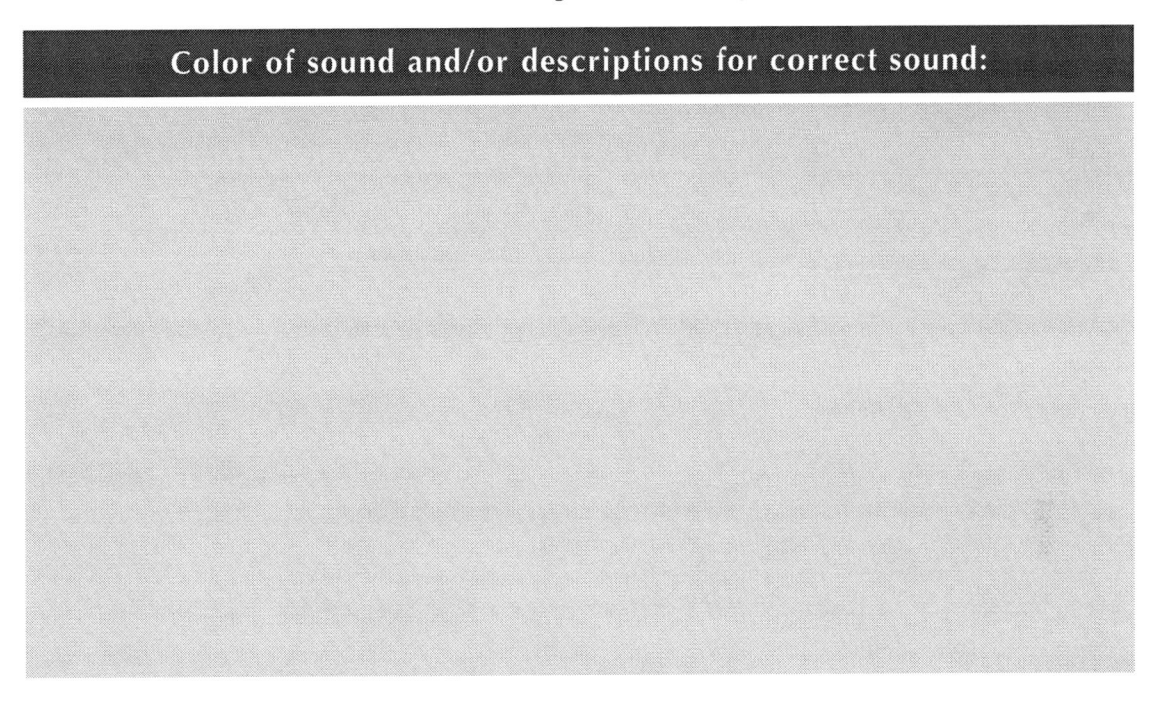

Color of sound and/or descriptions for correct sound:

Track 37   Exercise 6, Register Consistency with Downward Leaps (Incorrect)
Problem = altos sing in chest on downward leaps

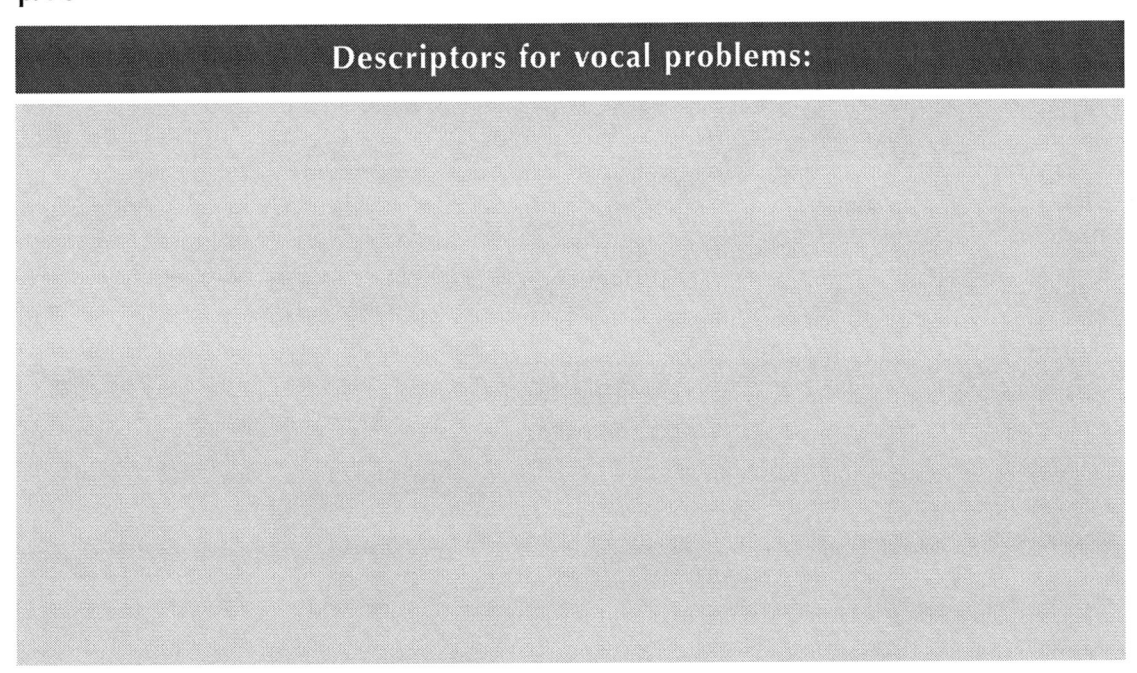

p. 76

Descriptors for vocal problems:

The Choral Conductor's Aural Tutor • James Jordan

pp. 53, 143

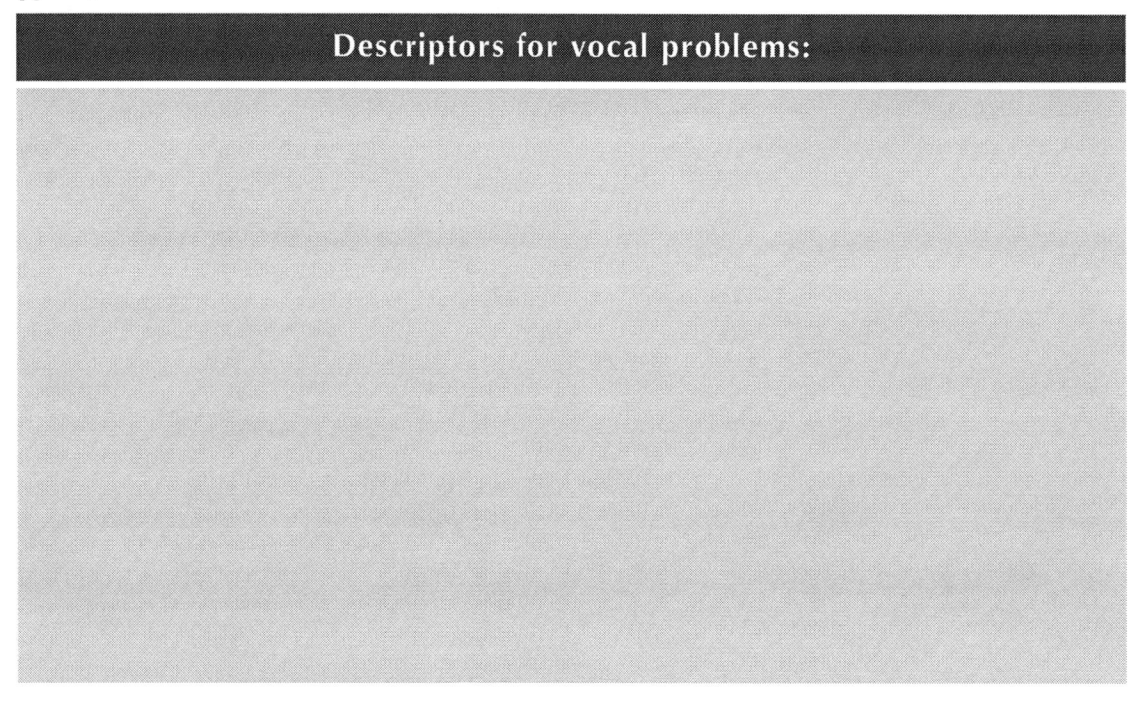

TRACK 38   Exercise 6, Register Consistency with Downward Leaps (Incorrect)
Problem = male voices sing with back jowl placement

Descriptors for vocal problems:

TRACK 39   Exercise 8, Range Extension Downward (Correct)

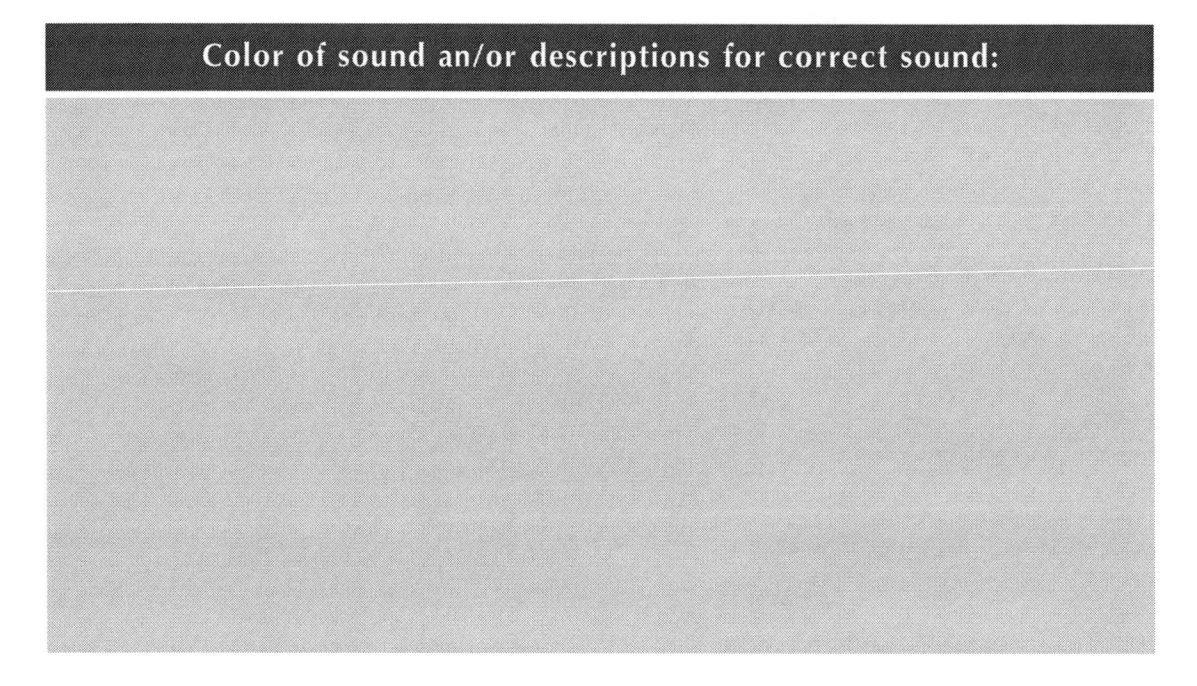

Color of sound an/or descriptions for correct sound:

Section Five: The Conductor's Aural Workbook

TRACK 40 Exercise 9, Range Extension Upward and Maintaining
On-the-Breath Singing (Correct)

Color of sound an/or descriptions for correct sound:

TRACK 41 Exercise 9, Range Extension Upward and Maintaining
On-the-Breath Singing (Incorrect)

pp. 50, 83, 108–109 Problem = no or little change in tongue position between
"oo" and "ee" vowels

Descriptors for vocal problems:

TRACK 42   Exercise 13, Upward Leaps on the Breath with Line; Listening (Correct)

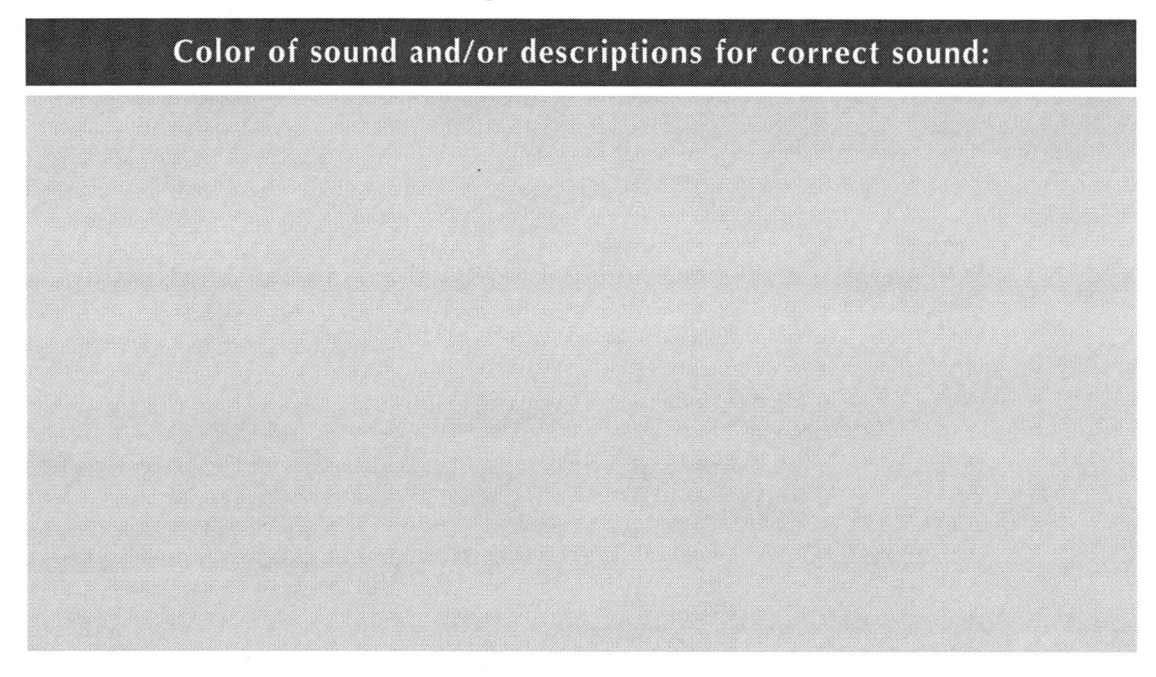

Color of sound and/or descriptions for correct sound:

TRACK 43   Exercise 14, Range Extension Upward (Correct)

Color of sound and/or descriptions for correct sound:

Section Five: The Conductor's Aural Workbook

TRACK 44 — Exercise 14, Range Extension Upward (Incorrect)
Problem = entire exercise off the breath

pp. 69, 147

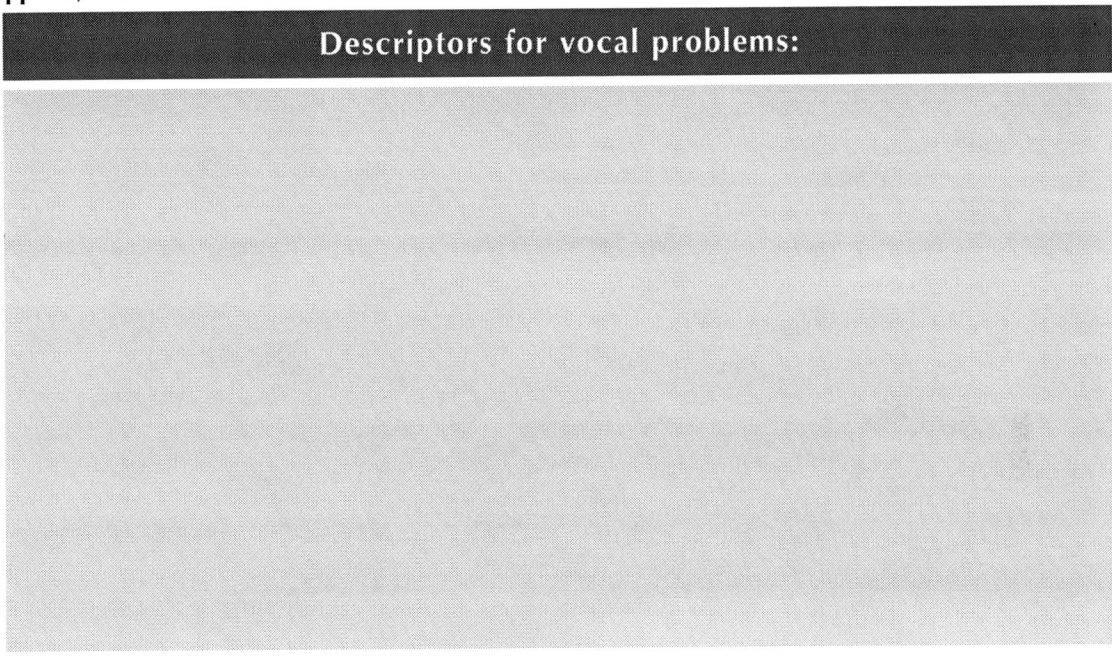

Descriptors for vocal problems:

TRACK 45 — Exercise 14, Range Extension Upward (Incorrect)
Problem = entire exercise sung with excessively open vowels

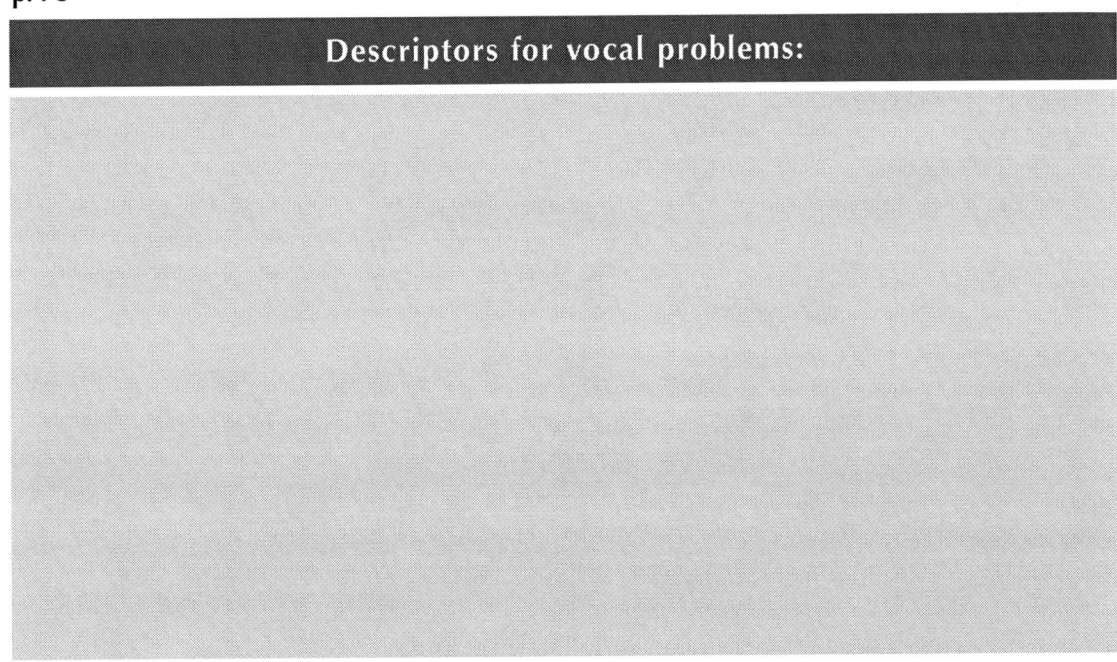

p. 78

Descriptors for vocal problems:

TRACK 46　　　Exercise 17, Making Space on Upward Leap;
　　　　　　　Vowel Modification (Correct)

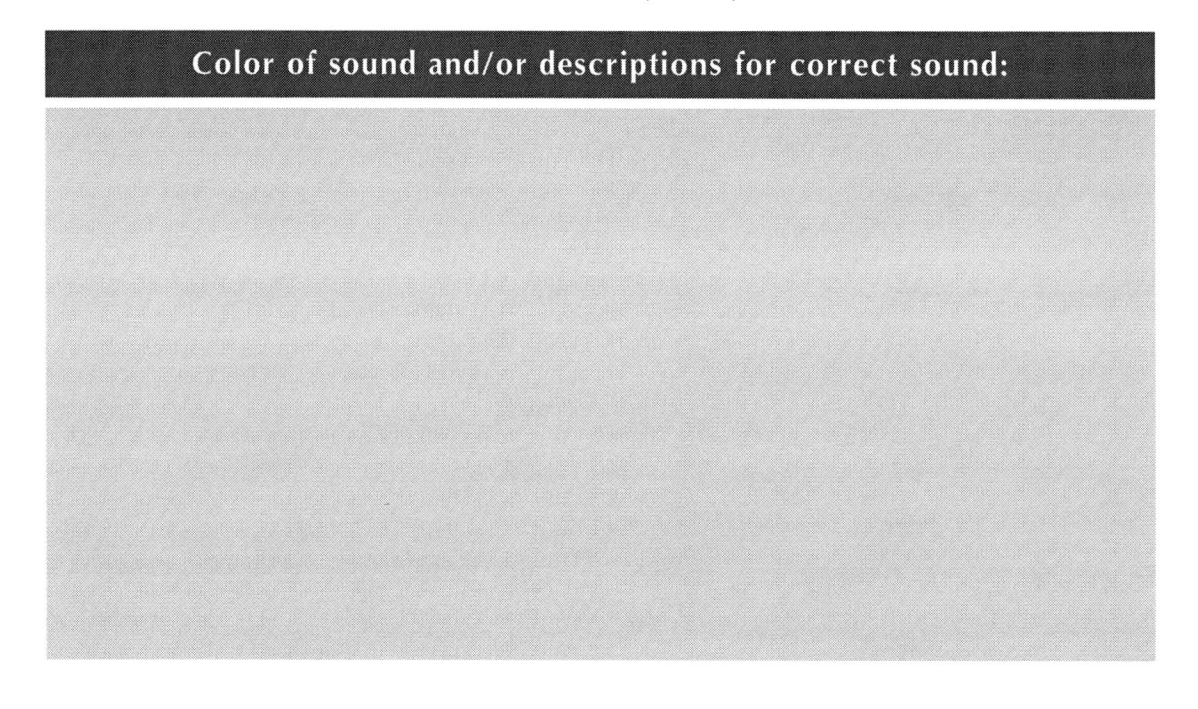

Color of sound and/or descriptions for correct sound:

pp. 63–67, 69

TRACK 47　　　Exercise 17, Making Space on Upward Leap;
　　　　　　　Vowel Modification (Incorrect)
　　　　　　　Problem = entire exercise off the breath

Descriptors for vocal problems:

Section Five: The Conductor's Aural Workbook

TRACK 48 — Exercise 17, Making Space on Upward Leap, Vowel Modification (Incorrect)

pp. 63–67, 69

Problem = initial note is sung on breath and rest of exercise is off the breath

Descriptors for vocal problems:

TRACK 49 — Exercise 17, Making Space on Upward Leap: Vowel Modification (Incorrect)

p. 53

Problem = men are singing with back placement or "jowl" vowels

Descriptors for vocal problems:

The Choral Conductor's Aural Tutor • James Jordan

pp. 53, 76

TRACK 50   Exercise 17, Making Space on Upward Leap;
Vowel Modification (Incorrect)
Problem = women are singing with back placement or "jowl" vowels

Descriptors for vocal problems:

TRACK 51   Exercise 18, Range Extension (Correct)

Color of sound and/or descriptions for correct sound:

Section Five: The Conductor's Aural Workbook

TRACK 52　　Exercise 18, Range Extension (Incorrect)
　　　　　　　Problem = no space made for upward leaps

p. 94

Descriptors for vocal problems:

TRACK 53　　Exercise 18, Range Extension (Incorrect)
　　　　　　　Problem = sung on breath but with open vowels

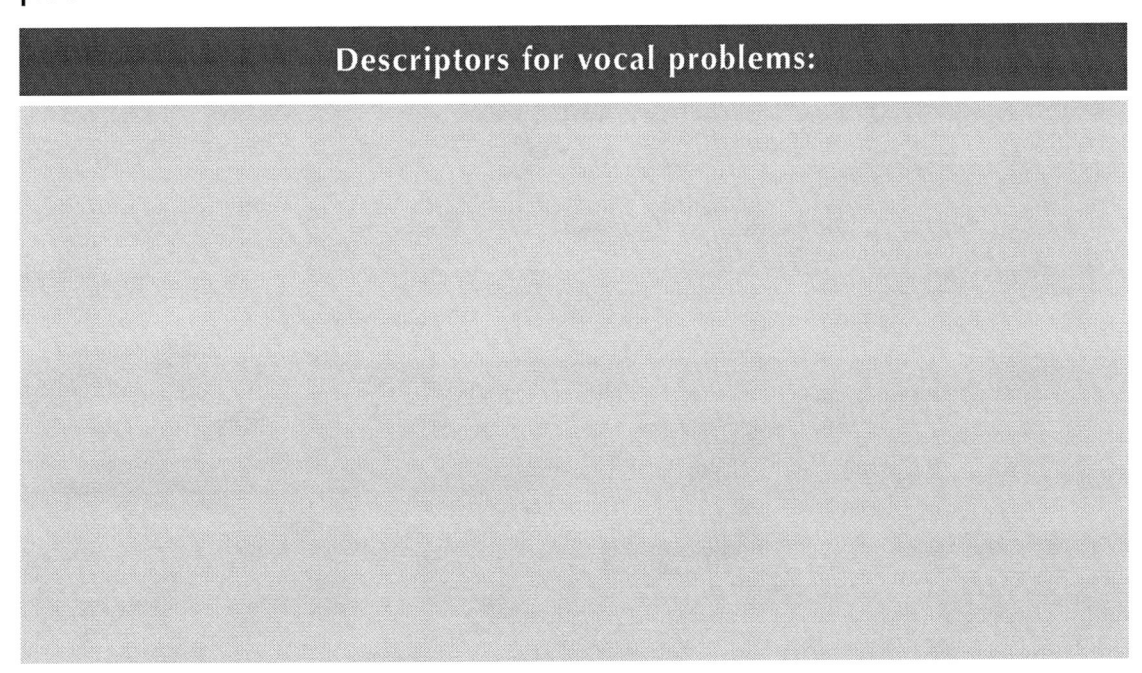

p. 78

Descriptors for vocal problems:

TRACK 54   Exercise 19, *Martellato* (Correct)

pp. 98–102

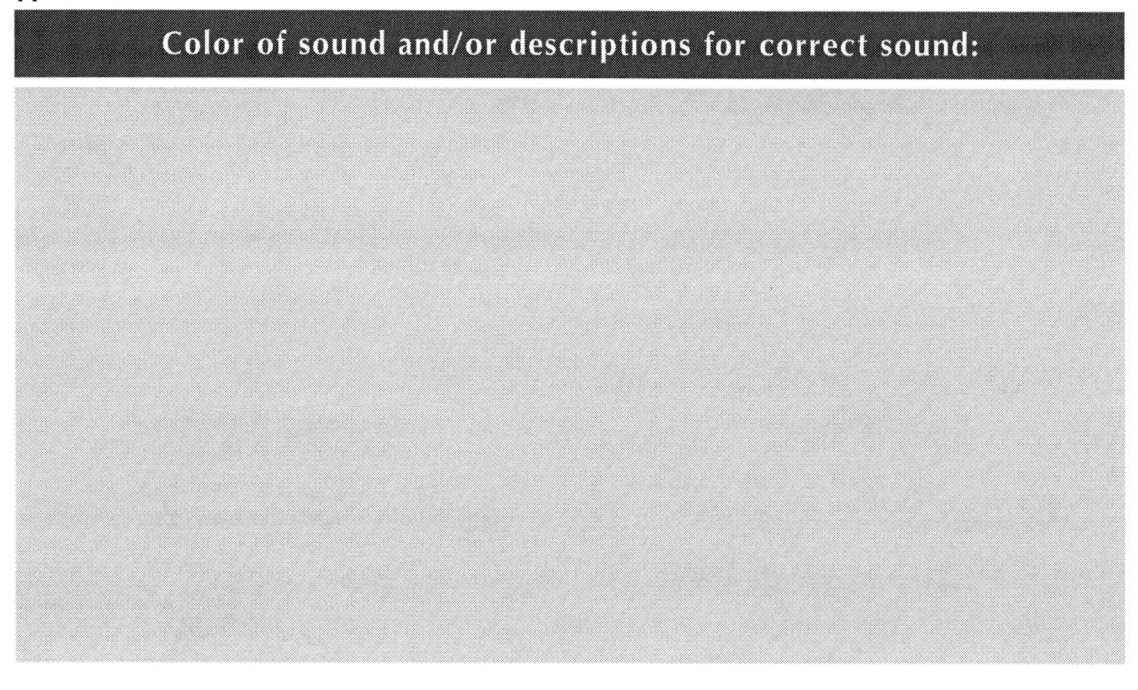

Color of sound and/or descriptions for correct sound:

TRACK 55   Sigh on "OO" (Correct)

pp. 12, 49–50, 59

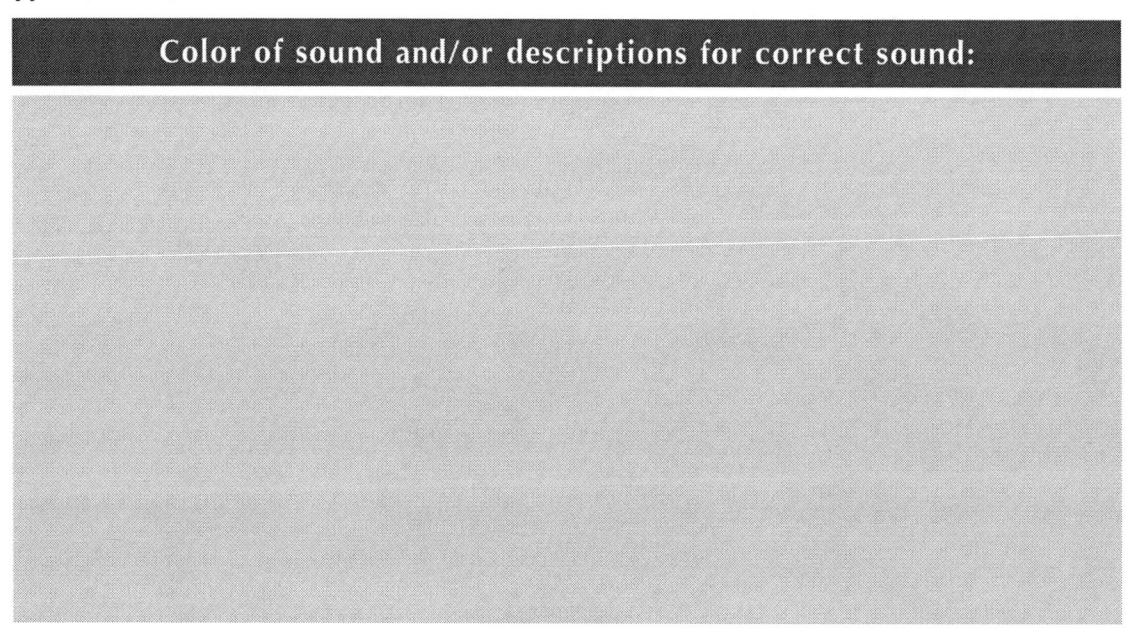

Color of sound and/or descriptions for correct sound:

Section Five: The Conductor's Aural Workbook

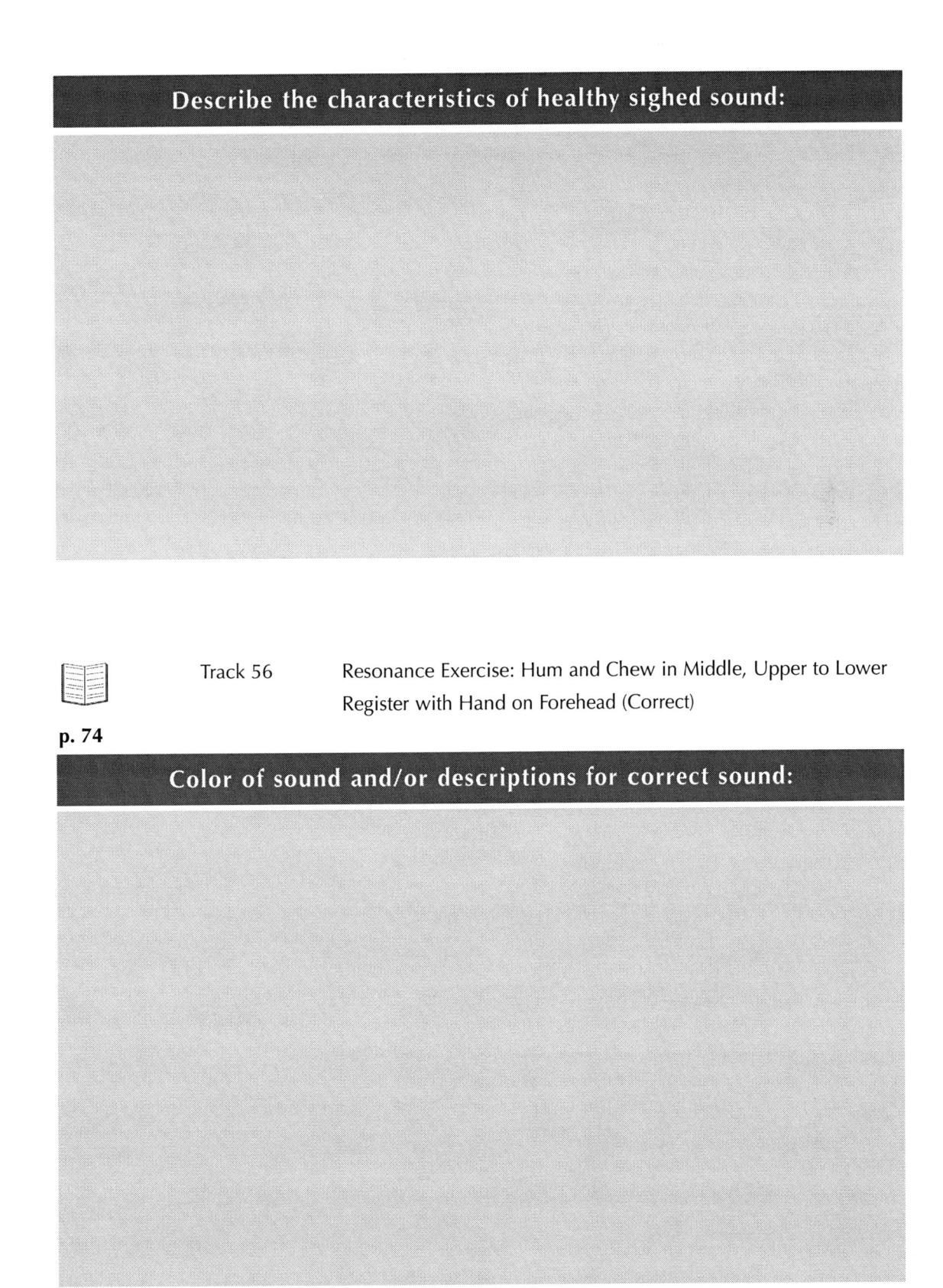

Describe the characteristics of healthy sighed sound:

Track 56   Resonance Exercise: Hum and Chew in Middle, Upper to Lower Register with Hand on Forehead (Correct)

p. 74

Color of sound and/or descriptions for correct sound:

Describe the sound of a healthy ensemble "hum and chew":

CD 2: The Pennsbury High School Chamber Choir

Accompanist Suggestions: Marilyn Shenenberger

Track Description

1. Introduction: Marilyn Shenenberger
2. Performing modulations: Marilyn Shenenberger—Short performing specifies for each of the Core Vocal Exercises performed on this CD with the choirs. Please note that incorrect performances also have incorrectly played accompaniments.
3. Accompanist performing specifics: Exercise 1 explanation
4. Accompanist performing specifics: Exercise 1 accompaniment
5. Accompanist performing specifics: Exercise 2 explanation
6. Accompanist performing specifics: Exercise 2 accompaniment
7. Accompanist performing specifics: Exercise 3 explanation
8. Accompanist performing specifics: Exercise 3 accompaniment
9. Accompanist performing specifics: Exercise 5 explanation
10. Accompanist performing specifics: Exercise 5 accompaniment
11. Accompanist performing specifics: Exercise 6 explanation
12. Accompanist performing specifics: Exercise 6 accompaniment
13. Accompanist performing specifics: Exercise 8 explanation
14. Accompanist performing specifics: Exercise 8 accompaniment
15. Accompanist performing specifics: Exercise 9 explanation
16. Accompanist performing specifics: Exercise 9 accompaniment
17. Accompanist performing specifics: Exercise 13 explanation
18. Accompanist performing specifics: Exercise 13 accompaniment
19. Accompanist performing specifics: Exercise 14 explanation
20. Accompanist performing specifics: Exercise 14 accompaniment
21. Accompanist performing specifics: Exercise 17 explanation
22. Accompanist performing specifics: Exercise 17 accompaniment
23. Accompanist performing specifics: Exercise 18 explanation
24. Accompanist performing specifics: Exercise 18 accompaniment
25. Accompanist performing specifics: Exercise 19 explanation
26. Accompanist performing specifics: Exercise 19 accompaniment
27. Accompanist performing specifics: Exercise 24 explanation
28. Accompanist performing specifics: Exercise 24 accompaniment
29. Comments on incorrect tracks and accompaniment on incorrect tracks

Exercises and Notebook for The Pennsbury Chamber Choir

TRACK 30   Exercise 1, Legato; Line (Correct)

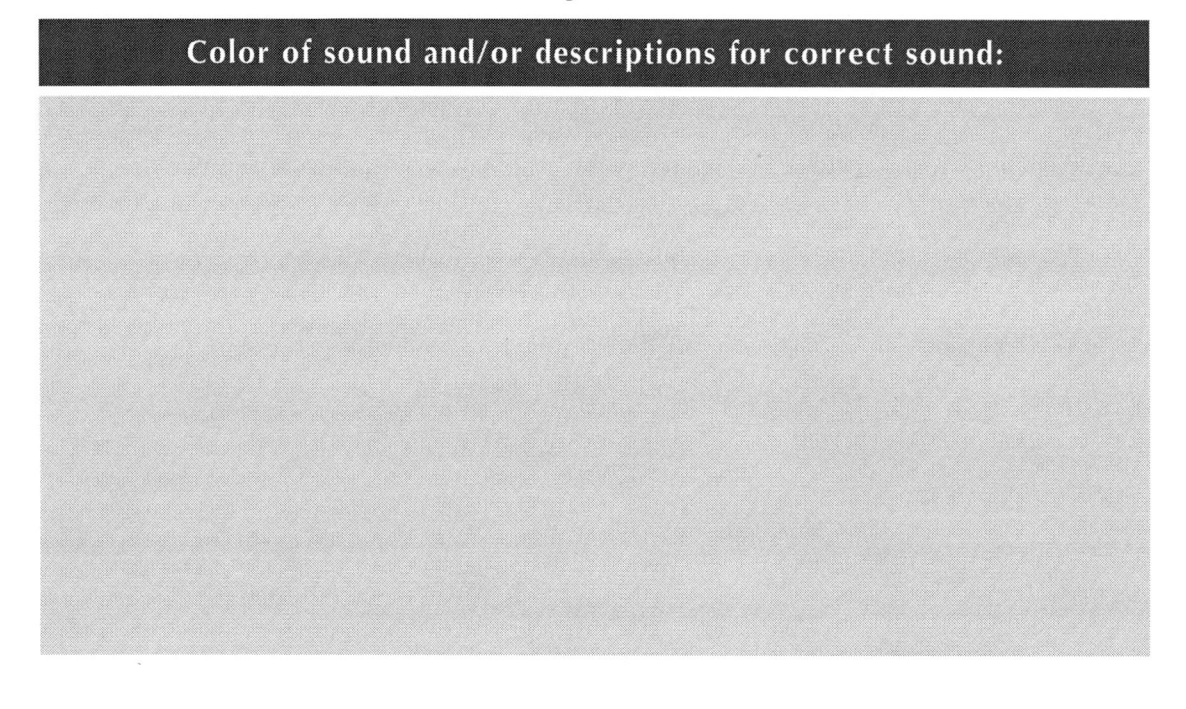

Color of sound and/or descriptions for correct sound:

TRACK 31   Exercise 1, Legato; Line (Incorrect)

Problem = women sing with little head tone in sound

p. 76

Descriptors for vocal problems:

Section Five: The Conductor's Aural Workbook

TRACK 32 Exercise 2, Repeated Tone with *Crescendo/Decrescendo* (Correct)

Color of sound and/or descriptions for correct sound:

TRACK 33 Exercise 2, Repeated Tone with *Crescendo/Decrescendo* (Incorrect)

pp. 94–95, 136 Problem = sluggish movement to vowel

Descriptors for vocal problems:

The Choral Conductor's Aural Tutor • James Jordan

TRACK 34   Exercise 5, Singing on Breath through Moving Eighth Notes (Correct)

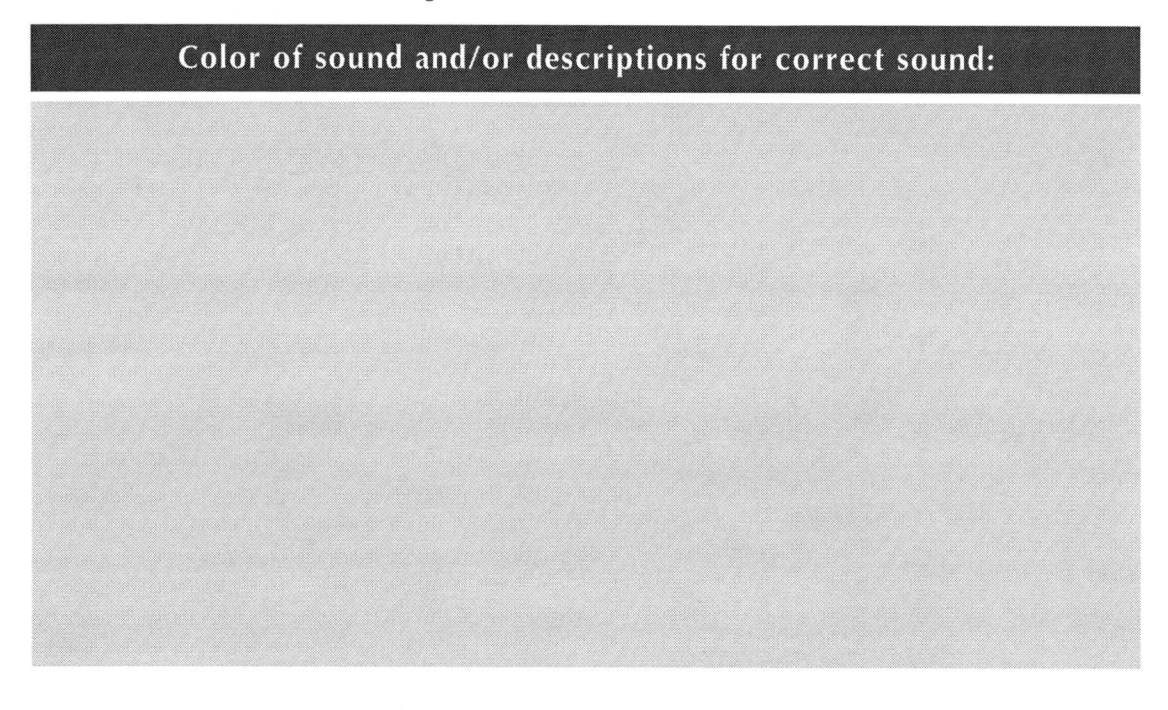

Color of sound and/or descriptions for correct sound:

TRACK 35   Exercise 5, Singing on Breath through Moving Eighth Notes (Incorrect)

pp. 83, 108–109   Problem = tongue position for "ee" vowel is not high enough

Descriptors for vocal problems:

Section Five: The Conductor's Aural Workbook

TRACK 36　　　Exercise 6, Register Consistency with Downward Leaps (Correct)

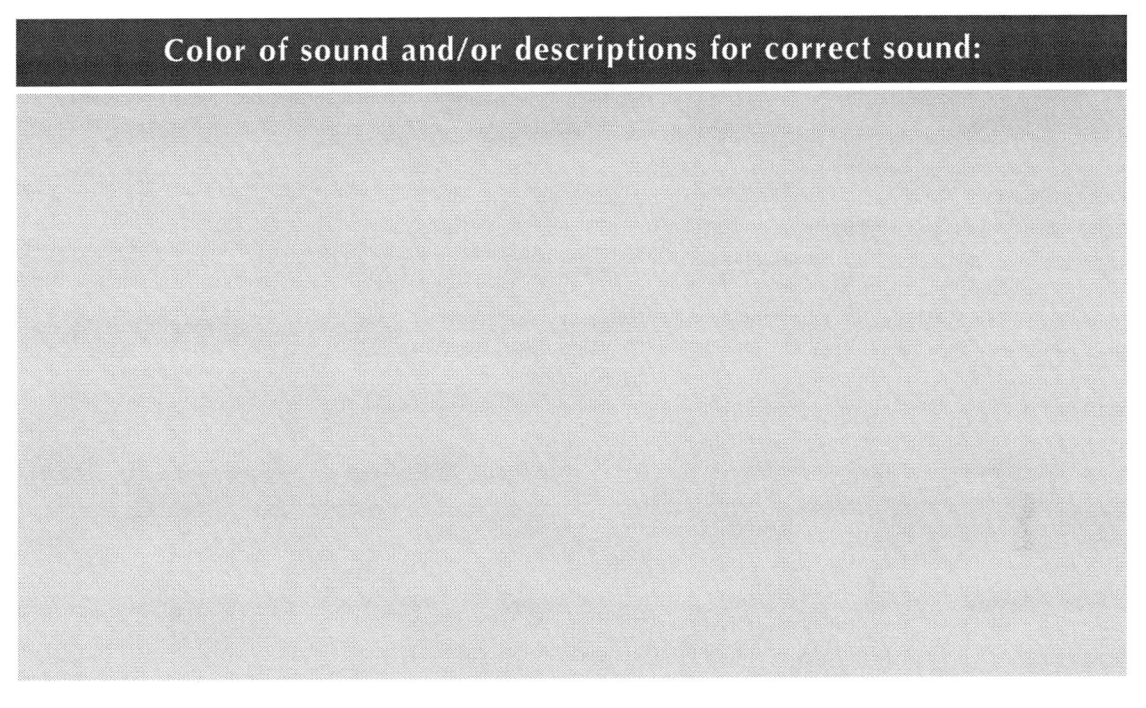

Color of sound and/or descriptions for correct sound:

p. 76

TRACK 37　　　Exercise 6, Register Consistency with Downward Leaps (Incorrect)
Problem = altos sing in chest on downward leaps

Descriptors for vocal problems:

The Choral Conductor's Aural Tutor • James Jordan

pp. 53, 143

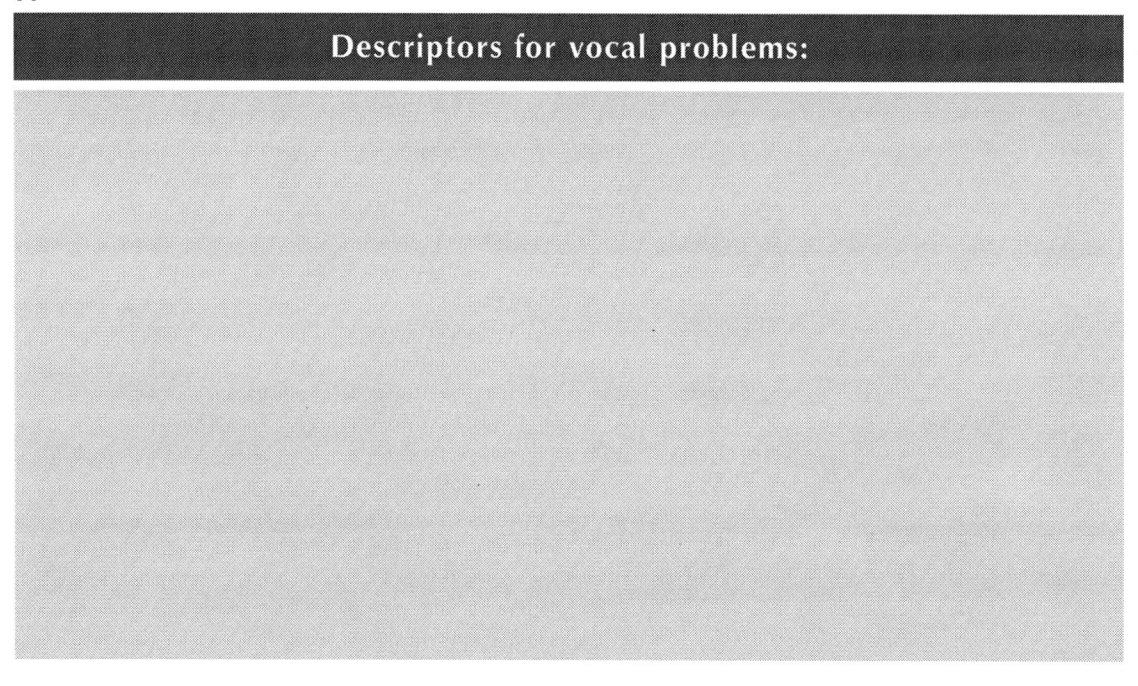

TRACK 38   Exercise 6, Register Consistency with Downward Leaps (Incorrect)
             Problem = Male voices sing with back "jowl" placement

Descriptors for vocal problems:

TRACK 39   Exercise 8, Range Extension Downward (Correct)

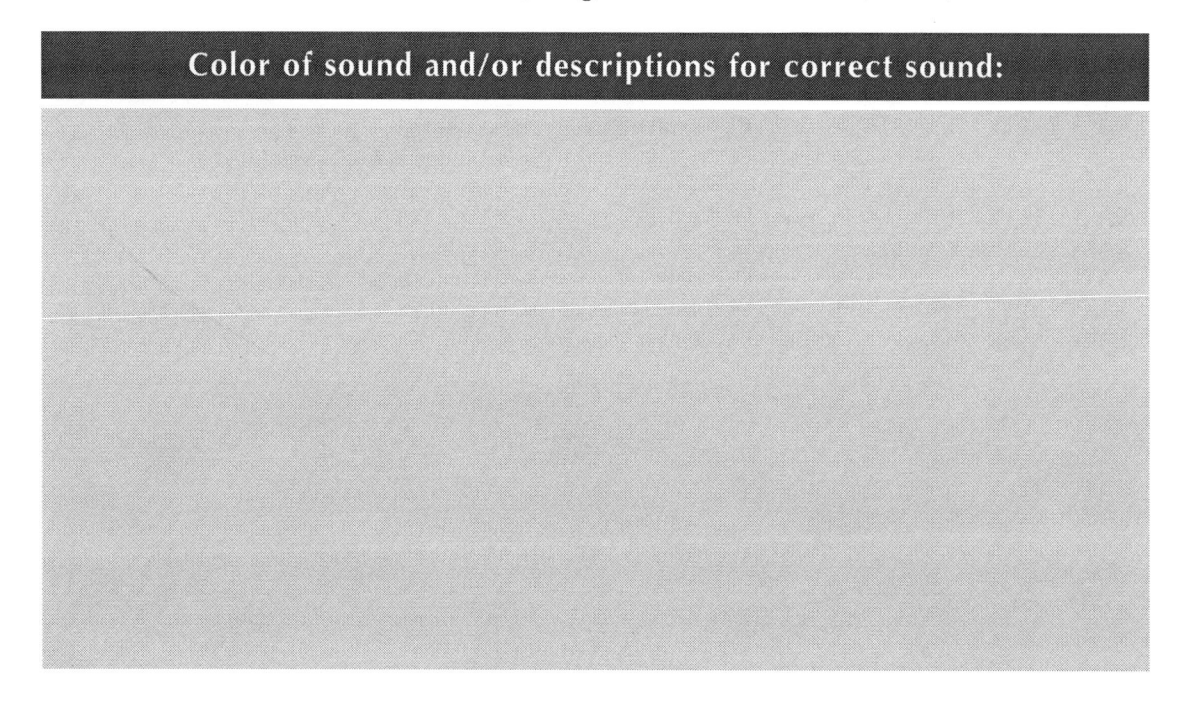

Color of sound and/or descriptions for correct sound:

82

Section Five: The Conductor's Aural Workbook

TRACK 40 Exercise 9, Range Extension Upward and Maintaining
On-the-Breath Singing (Correct)

Color of sound and/or descriptions for correct sound:

TRACK 41 Exercise 9, Range Extension Upward and Maintaining
On-the-Breath Singing (Incorrect)

pp. 50, 83, 108–109 Problem = No or little change in tongue position between "oo" and "ee" vowels

Descriptors for vocal problems:

83

TRACK 42   Exercise 13, Upward Leaps on the Breath with Line; Listening (Correct)

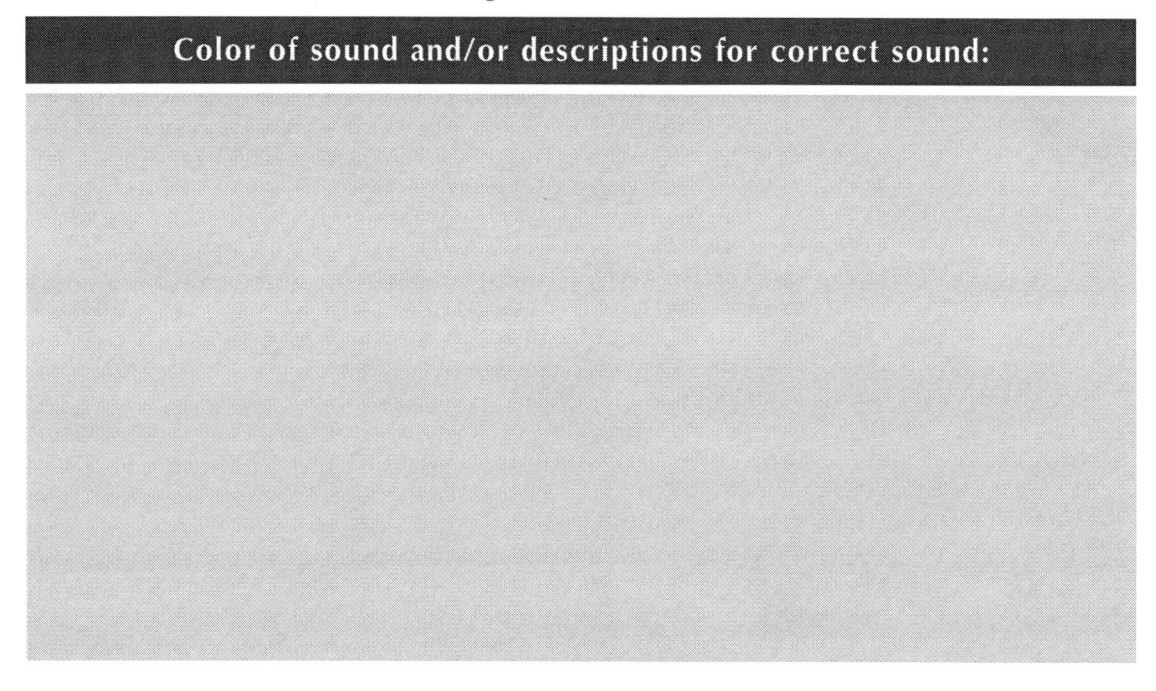

Color of sound and/or descriptions for correct sound:

TRACK 43   Exercise 14, Range Extension Upward (Correct)

Color of sound and/or descriptions for correct sound:

Section Five: The Conductor's Aural Workbook

TRACK 44   Exercise 14, Range Extension Upward (Incorrect)
            Problem = entire exercise off the breath

pp. 69, 147

Descriptors for vocal problems:

TRACK 45   Exercise 14, Range Extension Upward (Incorrect)
            Problem = entire exercise sung with excessively open vowels

p. 78

Descriptors for vocal problems:

TRACK 46 Exercise 17, Making Space on Upward Leap;
Vowel Modification (Correct)

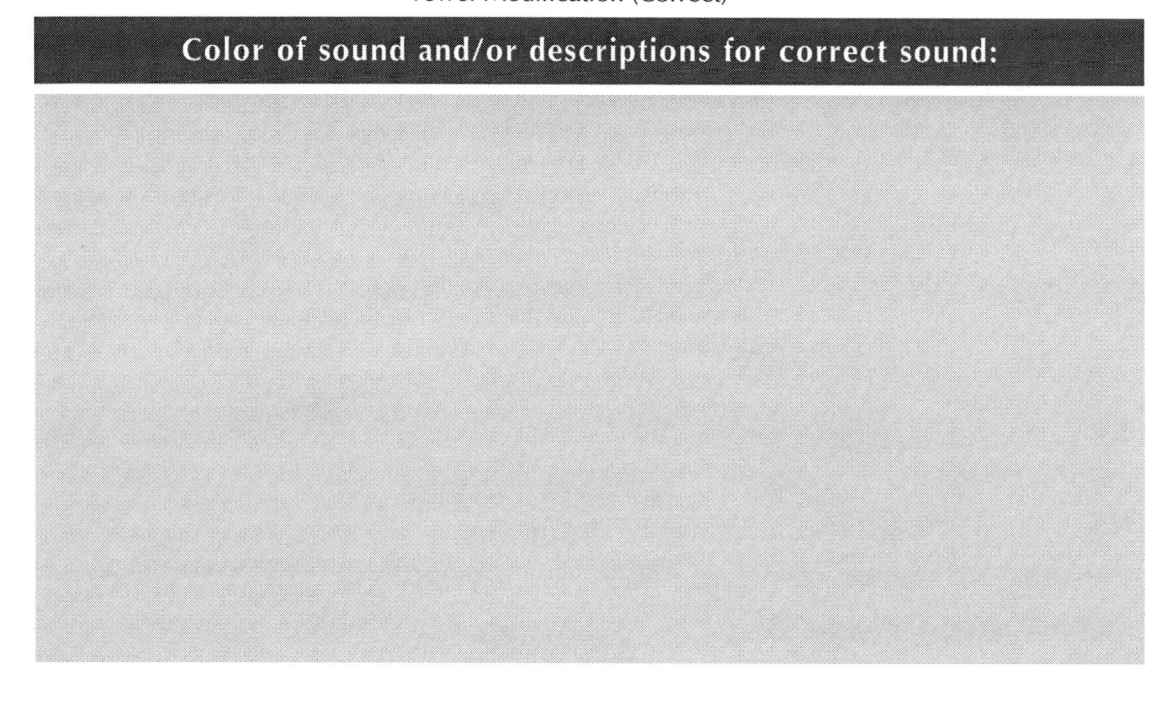

Color of sound and/or descriptions for correct sound:

TRACK 47 Exercised 17, Making Space on Upward Leap;
Vowel Modification (Incorrect)

pp. 63–67, 69 Problem = entire exercise off the breath

Descriptors for vocal problems:

Section Five: The Conductor's Aural Workbook

TRACK 48 — Exercise 17, Making Space on Upward Leap; Vowel Modification (Incorrect)

pp. 63–67, 69

Problem = only notes on upward leap are off the breath

Descriptors for vocal problems:

TRACK 49 — Exercise 17, Making Space on Upward Leap; Vowel Modification (Incorrect)

pp. 63–67, 69

Problem = initial note is sung on the breath and rest of exercise is off the breath

Descriptors for vocal problems:

The Choral Conductor's Aural Tutor • James Jordan

	TRACK 50	Exercise 17, Making Space on Upward Leap; Vowel Modification (Incorrect)
p. 53		Problem = men are singing with back placement or "jowl" vowels

Descriptors for vocal problems:

	TRACK 51	Exercise 17, Making Space on Upward Leap; Vowel Modification (Incorrect)
pp. 53, 76		Problem = women are singing with back placement or "jowl" vowels

Descriptors for vocal problems:

Section Five: The Conductor's Aural Workbook

TRACK 52   Exercise 18, Range Extension (Correct)

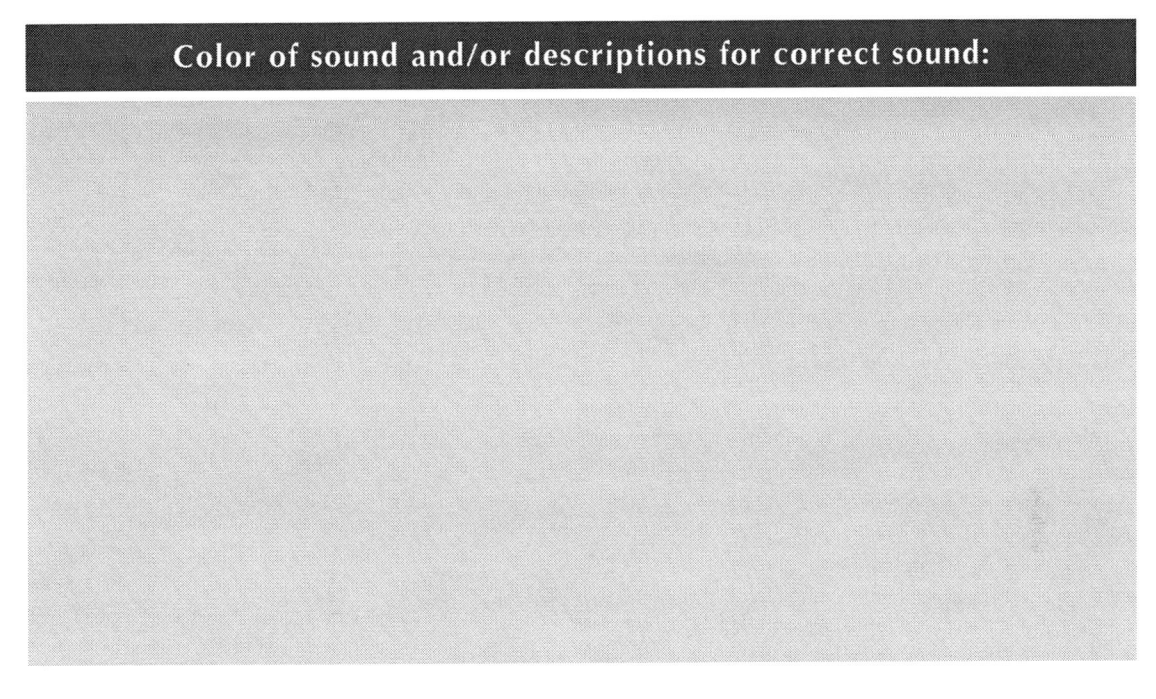

Color of sound and/or descriptions for correct sound:

TRACK 53   Exercise 18, Range Extension (Incorrect)
Problem = no space made for upward leaps

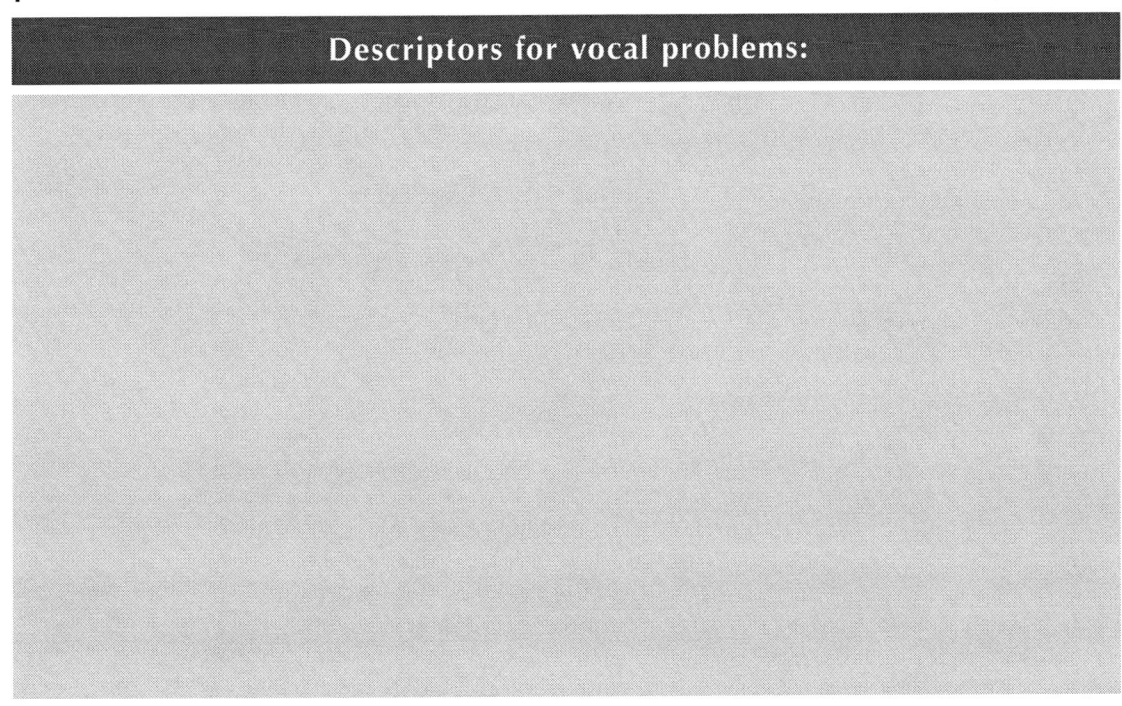

p. 94

Descriptors for vocal problems:

The Choral Conductor's Aural Tutor • James Jordan

p. 78

TRACK 54   Exercise 18, Range Extension (Incorrect)
Problem = sung on breath but with open vowels

Descriptors for vocal problems:

pp. 98–102

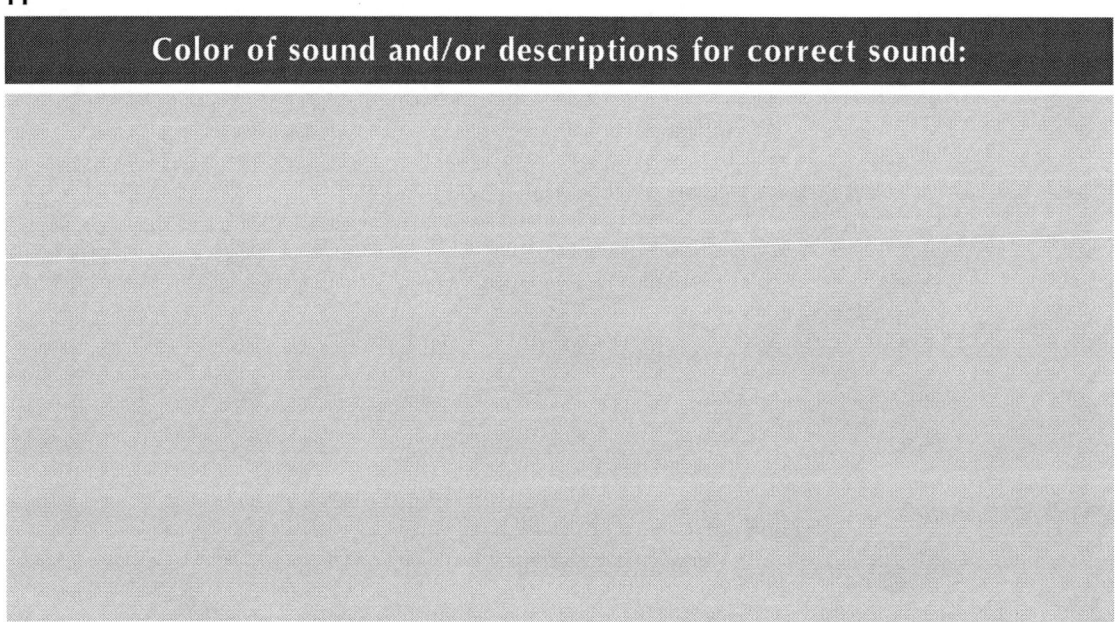

TRACK 55   Exercise 19, *Martellato* (Correct)

Color of sound and/or descriptions for correct sound:

Section Five: The Conductor's Aural Workbook

TRACK 56   Sigh on "OO" (Correct)

pp. 12, 49–50, 59

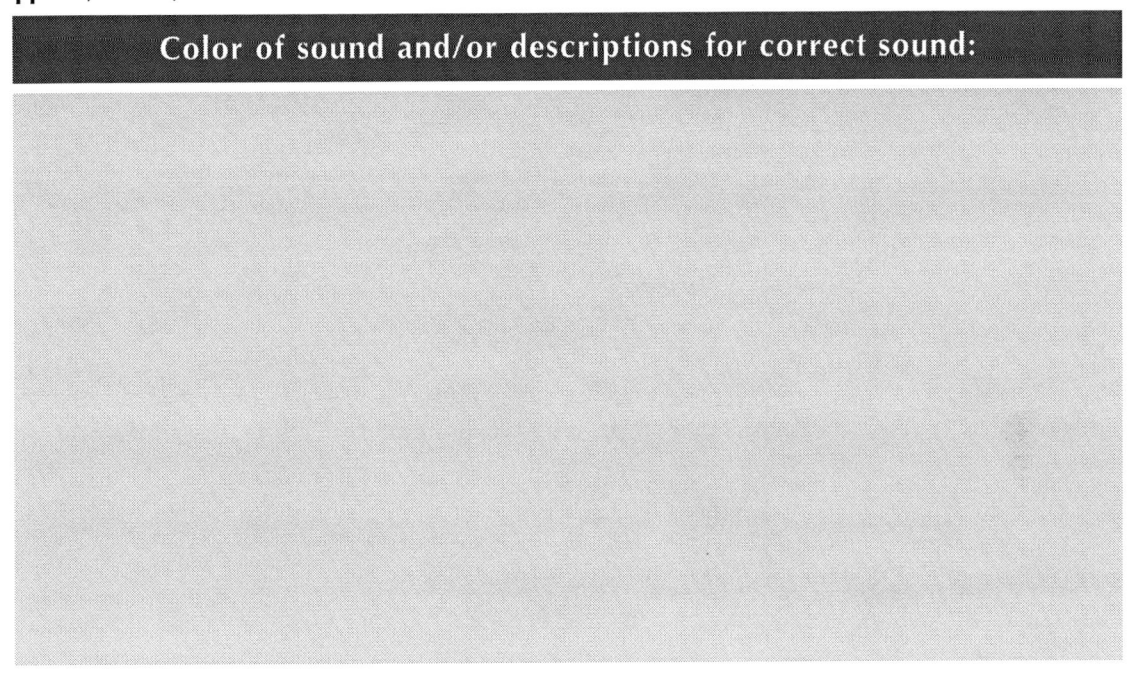

Color of sound and/or descriptions for correct sound:

TRACK 57   Resonance Exercise: Hum and Chew in Middle and Upper to Low Register with Hand on Forehead (Correct)

p. 74

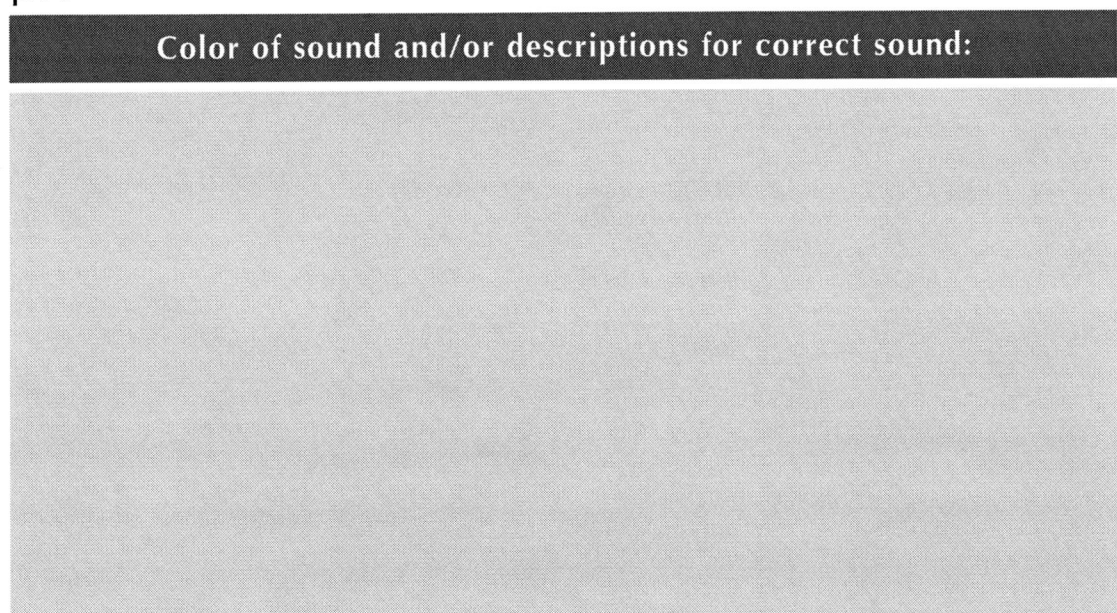

Color of sound and/or descriptions for correct sound:

SECTION SIX
PRETESTS AND POSTTESTS

Instructions (CD 1, Track 57)

You should take the following test twice before you begin this program of study and again after you have completed the program. Listen to each example, and mark the best answer for each question. Once the test has begun, do not stop playing the test to contemplate answers. It is suggested that you go with your first response and immediately circle your answer. Listen to each example. Immediately make a decision concerning what you hear. Again, do not stop the CD to ponder the answer. It is best to go with your first impulse. You must take the pretest twice in the same sitting to gain valuable results.

Remember: Take both Exam One and Exam Two in the same test session. Always take the test with headphones. The test is printed three times for your use and convenience.

A Note on Retaking the Test

I have been asked whether retaking the same test several times allows you to "learn" the correct answers through repetition of the test. This is, indeed, possible. However, this problem can be countered in two ways. First, allow for a considerable amount of time between taking the pretest and the posttest, as much as one week, if possible. Before taking the test the second time, focus intently on many listening repetitions on the items in which you experienced deficiencies. Repeatedly listen to the correct example. Remember that the ability to diagnose these issues rests with your ability to retain correct sounds within your ear. That can only be obtained through repeated listening. Focus on one vocal issue at a time. Do not go through all the problem questions and then repeat the list again. Repeated listening to one example will yield better results. Another option is to take the exam without paper. Select examples by randomly scanning track numbers. Verbally answer the musical examples, and then look at the track number and compare your answers to those in the workbook.

Pretest (Exam One)

The test starts on CD 1, track 58.

Circle the best answer.

1. a. Vowel sounds all open
   b. Vowel sounds not high and forward enough
   c. Entire exercise off the breath
   d. Exercise sung correctly

2. a. Altos sing in chest
   b. Vowels too open
   c. Entire exercise off the breath
   d. Exercise sung correctly

3. a. Altos sing in chest
   b. Vowels too open
   c. Entire exercise off the breath
   d. Exercise sung correctly

4. a. Altos sing in chest
   b. Vowels too open
   c. Entire exercise off the breath
   d. Exercise sung correctly

5. a. Altos sing in chest
   b. Vowels too open
   c. Entire exercise off the breath
   d. Exercise sung correctly

6. a. Women singing with back placement or "jowl" vowels
   b. Vowels too open
   c. Vowels too closed
   d. Exercise sung correctly

Section Six: Pretests and Posttests

7. a. Women singing with back placement or "jowl" vowels
   b. Vowels too open
   c. Vowels too closed
   d. Exercise sung correctly

8. a. Exercise off the breath
   b. Vowels too open
   c. Vowels too closed
   d. Exercise sung correctly

9. a. Men sing with "jowl" vowels
   b. Women sing with little head tone in sound
   c. Women sing with open vowels
   d. Exercise sung correctly

10. a. Men sing with "jowl" vowels
    b. Women sing with little head tone in sound
    c. No change in tongue position between "oo" and "ee" vowels
    d. Exercise sung correctly

11. a. No change in tongue position between "oo" and "ee" vowels
    b. Vowels too open
    c. Vowels too closed
    d. Exercise sung correctly

12. a. Men sing with "jowl" vowels
    b. Women sing with little head tone in sound
    c. No change in tongue position between "oo" and "ee" vowels
    d. Exercise sung correctly

13. a. Exercise off the breath
    b. Vowels too open
    c. Vowels too closed
    d. Exercise sung correctly

14. a. Exercise off the breath
    b. Vowels too open
    c. Vowels too closed
    d. Exercise sung correctly

15. a. Exercise off the breath
    b. Vowels too open
    c. Vowels too closed
    d. Exercise sung correctly

Section Six: Pretests and Posttests

Pretest (Exam Two)

The test starts on CD 1, track 58.

Circle the best answer.

1. a. Vowel sounds all open
   b. Vowel sounds not high and forward enough
   c. Entire exercise off the breath
   d. Exercise sung correctly

2. a. Altos sing in chest
   b. Vowels too open
   c. Entire exercise off the breath
   d. Exercise sung correctly

3. a. Altos sing in chest
   b. Vowels too open
   c. Entire exercise off the breath
   d. Exercise sung correctly

4. a. Altos sing in chest
   b. Vowels too open
   c. Entire exercise off the breath
   d. Exercise sung correctly

5. a. Altos sing in chest
   b. Vowels too open
   c. Entire exercise off the breath
   d. Exercise sung correctly

6. a. Women singing with back placement or "jowl" vowels
   b. Vowels too open
   c. Vowels too closed
   d. Exercise sung correctly

7. a. Women singing with back placement or "jowl" vowels
   b. Vowels too open
   c. Vowels too closed
   d. Exercise sung correctly

8. a. Exercise off the breath
   b. Vowels too open
   c. Vowels too closed
   d. Exercise sung correctly

9. a. Men sing with "jowl" vowels
   b. Women sing with little head tone in sound
   c. Women sing with open vowels
   d. Exercise sung correctly

10. a. Men sing with "jowl" vowels
    b. Women sing with little head tone in sound
    c. No change in tongue position between "oo" and "ee" vowels
    d. Exercise sung correctly

11. a. No change in tongue position between "oo" and "ee" vowels
    b. Vowels too open
    c. Vowels too closed
    d. Exercise sung correctly

12. a. Men sing with "jowl" vowels
    b. Women sing with little head tone in sound
    c. No change in tongue position between "oo" and "ee" vowels
    d. Exercise sung correctly

13. a. Exercise off the breath
    b. Vowels too open
    c. Vowels too closed
    d. Exercise sung correctly

14. a. Exercise off the breath
    b. Vowels too open
    c. Vowels too closed
    d. Exercise sung correctly

15. a. Exercise off the breath
    b. Vowels too open
    c. Vowels too closed
    d. Exercise sung correctly

Pretest (Exam Three)

The test starts on CD 1, track 58.

Circle the best answer.

1. a. Vowel sounds all open
    b. Vowel sounds not high and forward enough
    c. Entire exercise off the breath
    d. Exercise sung correctly

2. a. Altos sing in chest
    b. Vowels too open
    c. Entire exercise off the breath
    d. Exercise sung correctly

3. a. Altos sing in chest
    b. Vowels too open
    c. Entire exercise off the breath
    d. Exercise sung correctly

4. a. Altos sing in chest
    b. Vowels too open
    c. Entire exercise off the breath
    d. Exercise sung correctly

5. a. Altos sing in chest
    b. Vowels too open
    c. Entire exercise off the breath
    d. Exercise sung correctly

6. a. Women singing with back placement or "jowl" vowels
    b. Vowels too open
    c. Vowels too closed
    d. Exercise sung correctly

Section Six: Pretests and Posttests

7. a. Women singing with back placement or "jowl" vowels
   b. Vowels too open
   c. Vowels too closed
   d. Exercise sung correctly

8. a. Exercise off the breath
   b. Vowels too open
   c. Vowels too closed
   d. Exercise sung correctly

9. a. Men sing with "jowl" vowels
   b. Women sing with little head tone in sound
   c. Women sing with open vowels
   d. Exercise sung correctly

10. a. Men sing with "jowl" vowels
    b. Women sing with little head tone in sound
    c. No change in tongue position between "oo" and "ee" vowels
    d. Exercise sung correctly

11. a. No change in tongue position between "oo" and "ee" vowels
    b. Vowels too open
    c. Vowels too closed
    d. Exercise sung correctly

12. a. Men sing with "jowl" vowels
    b. Women sing with little head tone in sound
    c. No change in tongue position between "oo" and "ee" vowels
    d. Exercise sung correctly

13. a. Exercise off the breath
    b. Vowels too open
    c. Vowels too closed
    d. Exercise sung correctly

14. a. Exercise off the breath
    b. Vowels too open
    c. Vowels too closed
    d. Exercise sung correctly

15. a. Exercise off the breath
    b. Vowels too open
    c. Vowels too closed
    d. Exercise sung correctly

Posttest (Exam One)

The test starts on CD 1, track 58.

Circle the best answer.

1. a. Vowel sounds all open
    b. Vowel sounds not high and forward enough
    c. Entire exercise off the breath
    d. Exercise sung correctly

2. a. Altos sing in chest
    b. Vowels too open
    c. Entire exercise off the breath
    d. Exercise sung correctly

3. a. Altos sing in chest
    b. Vowels too open
    c. Entire exercise off the breath
    d. Exercise sung correctly

4. a. Altos sing in chest
    b. Vowels too open
    c. Entire exercise off the breath
    d. Exercise sung correctly

5. a. Altos sing in chest
    b. Vowels too open
    c. Entire exercise off the breath
    d. Exercise sung correctly

6. a. Women singing with back placement or "jowl" vowels
    b. Vowels too open
    c. Vowels too closed
    d. Exercise sung correctly

7. a. Women singing with back placement or "jowl" vowels
   b. Vowels too open
   c. Vowels too closed
   d. Exercise sung correctly

8. a. Exercise off the breath
   b. Vowels too open
   c. Vowels too closed
   d. Exercise sung correctly

9. a. Men sing with "jowl" vowels
   b. Women sing with little head tone in sound
   c. Women sing with open vowels
   d. Exercise sung correctly

10. a. Men sing with "jowl" vowels
    b. Women sing with little head tone in sound
    c. No change in tongue position between "oo" and "ee" vowels
    d. Exercise sung correctly

11. a. No change in tongue position between "oo" and "ee" vowels
    b. Vowels too open
    c. Vowels too closed
    d. Exercise sung correctly

12. a. Men sing with "jowl" vowels
    b. Women sing with little head tone in sound
    c. No change in tongue position between "oo" and "ee" vowels
    d. Exercise sung correctly

13. a. Exercise off the breath
    b. Vowels too open
    c. Vowels too closed
    d. Exercise sung correctly

14. a. Exercise off the breath
    b. Vowels too open
    c. Vowels too closed
    d. Exercise sung correctly

15. a. Exercise off the breath
    b. Vowels too open
    c. Vowels too closed
    d. Exercise sung correctly

Posttest (Exam Two)

The test starts on CD 1, track 58.

Circle the best answer.

1.
   a. Vowel sounds all open
   b. Vowel sounds not high and forward enough
   c. Entire exercise off the breath
   d. Exercise sung correctly

2.
   a. Altos sing in chest
   b. Vowels too open
   c. Entire exercise off the breath
   d. Exercise sung correctly

3.
   a. Altos sing in chest
   b. Vowels too open
   c. Entire exercise off the breath
   d. Exercise sung correctly

4.
   a. Altos sing in chest
   b. Vowels too open
   c. Entire exercise off the breath
   d. Exercise sung correctly

5.
   a. Altos sing in chest
   b. Vowels too open
   c. Entire exercise off the breath
   d. Exercise sung correctly

6.
   a. Women singing with back placement or "jowl" vowels
   b. Vowels too open
   c. Vowels too closed
   d. Exercise sung correctly

Section Six: Pretests and Posttests

7. a. Women singing with back placement or "jowl" vowels
   b. Vowels too open
   c. Vowels too closed
   d. Exercise sung correctly

8. a. Exercise off the breath
   b. Vowels too open
   c. Vowels too closed
   d. Exercise sung correctly

9. a. Men sing with "jowl" vowels
   b. Women sing with little head tone in sound
   c. Women sing with open vowels
   d. Exercise sung correctly

10. a. Men sing with "jowl" vowels
    b. Women sing with little head tone in sound
    c. No change in tongue position between "oo" and "ee" vowels
    d. Exercise sung correctly

11. a. No change in tongue position between "oo" and "ee" vowels
    b. Vowels too open
    c. Vowels too closed
    d. Exercise sung correctly

12. a. Men sing with "jowl" vowels
    b. Women sing with little head tone in sound
    c. No change in tongue position between "oo" and "ee" vowels
    d. Exercise sung correctly

13. a. Exercise off the breath
    b. Vowels too open
    c. Vowels too closed
    d. Exercise sung correctly

14. a. Exercise off the breath
　　b. Vowels too open
　　c. Vowels too closed
　　d. Exercise sung correctly

15. a. Exercise off the breath
　　b. Vowels too open
　　c. Vowels too closed
　　d. Exercise sung correctly

Posttest (Exam Three)

The test starts on CD 1, track 58.

Circle the best answer.

1. a. Vowel sounds all open
   b. Vowel sounds not high and forward enough
   c. Entire exercise off the breath
   d. Exercise sung correctly

2. a. Altos sing in chest
   b. Vowels too open
   c. Entire exercise off the breath
   d. Exercise sung correctly

3. a. Altos sing in chest
   b. Vowels too open
   c. Entire exercise off the breath
   d. Exercise sung correctly

4. a. Altos sing in chest
   b. Vowels too open
   c. Entire exercise off the breath
   d. Exercise sung correctly

5. a. Altos sing in chest
   b. Vowels too open
   c. Entire exercise off the breath
   d. Exercise sung correctly

6. a. Women singing with back placement or "jowl" vowels
   b. Vowels too open
   c. Vowels too closed
   d. Exercise sung correctly

7. a. Women singing with back placement or "jowl" vowels
   b. Vowels too open
   c. Vowels too closed
   d. Exercise sung correctly

8. a. Exercise off the breath
   b. Vowels too open
   c. Vowels too closed
   d. Exercise sung correctly

9. a. Men sing with "jowl" vowels
   b. Women sing with little head tone in sound
   c. Women sing with open vowels
   d. Exercise sung correctly

10. a. Men sing with "jowl" vowels
    b. Women sing with little head tone in sound
    c. No change in tongue position between "oo" and "ee" vowels
    d. Exercise sung correctly

11. a. No change in tongue position between "oo" and "ee" vowels
    b. Vowels too open
    c. Vowels too closed
    d. Exercise sung correctly

12. a. Men sing with "jowl" vowels
    b. Women sing with little head tone in sound
    c. No change in tongue position between "oo" and "ee" vowels
    d. Exercise sung correctly

13. a. Exercise off the breath
    b. Vowels too open
    c. Vowels too closed
    d. Exercise sung correctly

14. a. Exercise off the breath
    b. Vowels too open
    c. Vowels too closed
    d. Exercise sung correctly

15. a. Exercise off the breath
    b. Vowels too open
    c. Vowels too closed
    d. Exercise sung correctly

Pretest and Posttest Answers

Instructions for Scoring Your Tests

Score both tests. When you have completed the scoring, compare the answers on both tests. If you have mastered the content for some or all of the items, the answers will agree on both tests. If answers do not agree on separate tests, it indicates that you are not discriminating well on those items. Go back and study the workbook sections that address the incorrect responses again. For example, in question one, if you chose the answer "vowel sounds not high and forward enough," return to those items in the workbook that address on-the-breath sounds.

A Note on Scoring the Initial Tests

You are asked to take the test for this aural tutor twice in immediate succession. This is an important part of this workbook. After taking these tests, score both. If you score roughly the same on both tests, those results indicate that you are consistent, and that your answers reflect both strengths and the weaknesses in your knowledge. While you should then proceed through the entire workbook, you should pay particular attention to those areas you answered incorrectly.

If your scores varied greatly between both these tests, that result could be indicative of several issues. A wide difference between scores suggests that you were not certain of your answers and may have guessed about the sounds you were hearing. A wide difference in the scores between the tests would indicate that you are unsure as to what you heard. Careful study of the listening examples and careful completion of the workbook are required.

Correct Answers

1. *c.* Entire exercise off the breath
2. *d.* Exercise sung correctly (legato line)
3. *a.* Altos sing in chest (on downward leaps)
4. *b.* Vowels too open
5. *c.* Entire exercise off the breath
6. *a.* Women are singing with back placement or "jowl" vowels
7. *b.* Vowels too open
8. *d.* Exercise sung correctly
9. *b.* Women sing with little head tone in sound
10. *a.* Men sing with "jowl" vowels
11. *a.* No change in tongue position between "oo" and "ee" vowel
12. *a.* Men sing with "jowl" vowels
13. *d.* Exercise sung correctly (entirely on breath on moving eighth notes)
14. *a.* Exercise off the breath
15. *a.* Exercise off the breath

SECTION SEVEN

EXPANDING YOUR ABILITY TO HEAR CHORAL TEXTURES AND COLORS

Section Seven: Expanding Your Ability to Hear Choral Textures and Colors

Gaining More Listening Experiences for Choral Color: Hearing Resonances

When you have completed and mastered the preceding exercises, you have gained the understanding and the ability to hear the fundamental issues of vocal technique. From this point onward, because you have now acquired basic listening skills, diagnostic ensemble listening ability can be both developed and deepened through a program of listening study. I have always believed that your ability to hear all the other dimensions of choral performance outside the areas of pitch and rhythm are developed by a regular, self-imposed program of critical listening.

Setting Your Listening Priorities

As I stated earlier in this book, to develop a multidimensional listening sense, elements of pitch and rhythm must at some times be relegated to lower priorities in your listening schema. The finest voice teachers have ears that are finely tuned to hear the minutest changes in resonance or vocal color. Resonance is the keystone that leads one to other technical aspects: musical line, style, and issues of language color. From my perspective, the ability to hear choral color and texture is a central conducting skill. This ability can be developed and refined throughout one's musical career. Aside from providing valuable pedagogical insights, the ability to then take one's color sense and fantasize about color when deciding how best to represent a composer's voice is an invaluable skill for creating exciting and honest musical performances.

Hearing Musical Styles: Vocalic Flow and Mode

In trying to examine the various aspects of choral colors, the following mathematical analogy may be helpful.

Choral timbre = vocalic flow + modal color

vowel shape

I believe the ability to understand musical styles of historical periods and the color language or preferences of a particular composer rests on one's capability to hear choral colors. Language, or more specifically, the vowel, is the vehicle that carries color. The shape and resonance of vowels determine, in part, the choral style.[1] There can be no substitute for the understanding of the color of each language and the role of both consonants and vowels in those languages. However, the operative word to understanding musical style through language is "color," and this is determined by vowel shape within the parameters of each language.

Vocalic flow refers to the resonant continuity of the vowel, propelled by the breath of the singer. The ability to hear the continuity of vocalic flow and the inherent color of the resonance contained within vocalic flow is the major factor in hearing and tracking musical line. However, to hear a vowel moving forward is not enough. The vowel carries with it, at all times, vocal color. The ability to hear that color, describe it, and improve it should become the lot of the choral conductor's aural life.

Choral color is also determined by the mode of the music. This aspect of color is often overlooked by conductors because they identified the modes used in the composition or recognized that those modes have distinct and separate colors, e.g., phrygian creates a different palette than mixolydian. Part of unlocking the composer's intent is to know what modes were employed in the composition of the piece at hand.

In addition to the above color qualities, the modes also assume unique color characteristics within each historical music period and within each composer's idiomatic or non-idiomatic harmonic use of the modes. Hence, the color possibilities for their use are almost limitless, providing a vast color spectrum for the choral palette. The use of modes by Bruckner creates a vastly different world than the world related via modes in the music of Ives. An understanding of modes, combined with their historical context, provides a vast number of colors in the choral genre.[2]

---

[1]. Rhythmic issues are also intimately connected to musical style. While many musicological issues surround the correct performance practice of various periods, the focus of this book is color.

[2]. For a detailed description of modes and how to determine them via a step-by-step procedure, see *Choral Ensemble Intonation: Methods, Procedures, and Exercises* by James Jordan and Matthew Mehaffey, published by GIA Publications.

Gaining the Ability to Hear the Colors of the Modes

One way you can deepen your ability to perceive and hear color in choral sound is by training yourself to hear modally. The text *Ear Training Immersion Exercises for Choirs* can be the conductor's best friend in this regard. Singing each exercise and listening to the CD that accompanies the text encourage aural familiarity with the modes. Repeated listening and singing of the exercises will open doors to choral color that had been previously unknown. The text and accompanying recording should be used in combination with this text to educate one's ears for the choral rehearsal. As one listens to each mode presented in the text, the listener should attempt to categorize each mode by a color.

The Role of Visualization of Color and Its Effects upon Choral Sound

I cannot overemphasize the importance of developing a visual sense of color to assist musicians with fantasizing about color. An ability to visualize and fantasize about color transfers directly to ensemble sounds through vowel colors.

Too many times, I hear choirs that sing beautifully, but, to my ear, sound monochromatic at best. One color or a few limited colors pervade *all* the pieces they perform regardless of the style or harmonic content. The education of musicians could be enhanced through a study of color and texture in the art world. Regular viewing of the works of great artists should be part of the study diet of any conductor. I have spent a great deal of time looking at the works of James Duprée. Other great artists can likewise perform this valuable service. For example, the clarity and color of Mark Rothko juxtaposed with the density of Jackson Pollock can deepen the conductor's ability to fantasize about choral texture when translated into a parallel sound world. The following questions might help to organize and direct your viewing of any great painting.

1. How many different colors exist in this painting?

2. How many different shapes and sizes occur in this painting?

3. What is the most brilliant color in this painting, and where is it located?

4. Where is the richest hue in this painting?

5. How many different and distinct textures exist in this painting?

6. Is there a predominant color in this painting? If so, what is it?

7. Is there depth to the colors of this painting? Explain.

8. What is your favorite color in this painting? Might that color be the color "default" in your choral sound?

9. What is the most "unusual" or surprising color in this painting? Where is it located?

10. What color caught your eye first?

The Crayola School of Texture Education

The color world of great artists can be one catalyst and guide for conductors, and the lowly box of Crayolas can be the conductor's best friend. Many of my students have struggled with the concept of choral texture/color. Both words, texture and color, are synonyms. If one cannot visualize color to some degree, one may not be able to translate that color world into a sound world. These experiences, I feel, can be mutually dependent and mutually beneficial.

Have you ever watched a child with a large box of crayons? They pick their colors carefully and methodically. Each child has favorite colors. What makes a color one's favorite? If one, indeed, has a favorite color, is that the "default" color? Each child carefully chooses each color for the picture he or she is coloring. The process that the child goes through in creating a color world should probably be no different for a musician. As children, our art world was the world we lived in, a world of colors and textures. As we grow older and more "mature" that fantasy sense disappears or abates unless we stimulate our visual senses. Perhaps, just perhaps, a return to the world of crayons may be enough to jolt us out of our bland textural worlds!

After score study I have had students describe the sound of the work or sections of that work by selecting colors from a box of crayons. It is always fascinating to see the diversity of opinions that range from bland to outrageous within a class. After discussions about style and text meaning, the color selections usually become more consistent across the class. I then ask the students to select at least three colors that represent the piece they are to conduct and to color the staves with those colors.

The change in their music making is always profound. In part, this is because a selection of a color, any color, affects both their breath and their gesture. The colors selected are mysteriously and magically transferred to the sound of the ensemble via the vowel and its color-carrying potential! I encourage each of you to become friends with a large box of crayons as part of your textural education.

Create an Inspiration Board or Collage for Pieces You Conduct

This is a technique I have learned from my artist friends. When they are ready to embark on a design project or a new work of art they assemble a collection of pictures, fabrics, and other objects that suggest both colors and textures for the creations they are about to tackle. Sometimes these inspiration boards contain only a few items, and sometimes they include many. Those small collected pictures, swatches, and other items serve as an initial color and textural blueprint for the new project.

For those who find fantasizing about color to be a problem, this may be an avenue worth pursuing. For each choral piece, assemble a collage of colors and textures that most closely resembles the textures you would like to achieve with your choir, and visualize them as you study each piece.

Tall and Narrow versus Rounder Resonances: Avoid Bright versus Dark

The primary focus of this text is to help you gain facility in hearing textures within a choral ensemble sound. After you have mastered the principles contained in this tutor, you may wish to gain further expertise in textural hearing through focused and self-directed listening study. While such expertise can be gathered throughout the rehearsal process, that process can be accelerated through aural study outside of the rehearsal room.

For many years, I categorized choral sound as either bright or dark. Those subjective terms tend to confound not only the technical aspects of the sound, but are also limited by one's individual perceptions of bright and dark. Both terms are highly subjective and open to a wide variety of

Section Seven: Expanding Your Ability to Hear Choral Textures and Colors

interpretations. Further, I have always believed that the use of "bright" and "dark" fails to address the essential elements of choral sound and confines definitions to a very narrow range. I have also found that the terms "bright" and "dark" are somewhat dangerous to employ in a choral rehearsal because of the inconsistency of the meaning of those words when translated in singers' minds.[3] How bright or how dark should a sound be?

The answer is relative to one's individual perception, which is in direct relationship to one's listening experience. Overly bright sounds may translate into sounds produced with a high larynx or excessively high palate. Sounds that are too dark may be the result of a "jowl" placement that is too far back or from a tension-ridden tongue. Both extremes must be avoided. Such terms seem to become the default words when one has not sufficiently considered all the issues involved with the resonances of vowel sounds.

I have found two approaches effective in further focusing thought concerning general resonance and have also provided an efficient pedagogical language for use in a choral ensemble. One approach is to ask the choir to either imagine a tall/narrow vowel or a round vowel.[4] By simply asking the choir to visualize the shape of the vowel, the appropriate resonances will be generated. Also, by using this approach you have begun to teach diction through appropriate vowel color.

The second approach is to affect vowel color with the temperature of the breath. For a brighter vowel color, ask the choir to take a cool breath. For a darker vowel color, ask the choir to take a warm breath. For the darker vowel colors, it may be helpful to once again ask the choir members to place the heel of their hands on their foreheads to ensure high and forward placement and avoid "jowl" vowels, which tend to lack resonance and cause pitch problems within the ensemble sound.

Both categories of colors, whether they are tall and narrow or round sounds, have a marked difference in how they sound to the conductor's ear. It is important to keep in mind that the choral ensemble color must be in the foreground of the conductor's aural world. Color must be the aspect of musical sound heard first, and it must be recognized and categorized by the

---

3. Meribeth Bunch, in her book *Dynamics of the Singing Voice*, presents a convincing argument as to why such terms as "bright" and "dark" create pedagogical and technical confusion in singers.

4. Note: In the warm-up, you must make a choice. If you do not, the choir will usually default to the vowel shape most closely associated with their speaking dialects! In *The Choral Warm-Up*, I spend considerable time explaining these concepts. Refer to the appropriate sections of that text for further information and clarification.

conductor. The conductor's ear must be trained to prioritize listening by constantly monitoring ensemble sound for vowel shape. Vigilance concerning the hearing of vowel shapes will reap tremendous rewards for the sound of the choir and will increase its ability to sing in tune. Changes in vowel shape are always the first indicators for a change in basic vocal production by the choir. The changes in vowel shape may be dramatic or quite subtle. The skillful conductor will be able to identify those subtle changes and then apply appropriate pedagogical steps for healthier singing by the ensemble.

I am advocating a listening sense that focuses upon hearing vowel sounds as the carriers of choral color and texture rather than both consonants and vowels. While consonants can either positively or negatively affect the vowel, it is the vocalic content of each vowel that creates the resonant ambiance of a choral sound. While consonants in choral ensembles define and clarify rhythm within a choral sound, it is the vowel that carries all things textural. An acute awareness of vowel-to-vowel movement within the musical line and the vertical texture of the choir can prove to be the conductor's most valuable tool. That ability to hear the vowel and all its subtleties points to the vocal pedagogical direction for the conductor. Further, the vocal health of a choral ensemble can only be diagnosed through vowel sounds. One must be careful to realize that other factors, such as pitch and rhythm, can mask more serious ensemble sound problems within the conductor's hearing world. The skill a conductor should strive to develop is a listening awareness of the shifting priorities at will during the course of a rehearsal. A nimble and aware ear is our goal. The way, I believe, to develop such a broad aural awareness is through the development of specific listening skills that focus on single aspects of choral ensemble sound.

The challenge of learning to hear the differences in these vowel colorations has been the subject of many student questions. Beyond the issues identified in this book, listening to CDs of various choral groups promotes a further "aural education." If one chooses to study choral sound in this manner, it will become necessary to reprioritize one's listening schema. That is, one must listen to the suggested recordings in Section Eight focusing on vowel shape (resonance). One should *not* critically listen to any of these recordings to evaluate any other musical elements of the performances. Focus only upon listening to vowel shapes!

SECTION EIGHT

RECOMMENDED LISTENING LIST FOR FURTHER AURAL ANALYSIS AND COLOR STUDY

Section Eight: Recommended Listening List for Further Aural Analysis and Color Study

Recommended Listening List for Further Aural Analysis and Color Study

Students frequently ask, "How can I improve my ability to listen and diagnose?" As I stated earlier in this text, this ability is built over time, and I believe improvements in one's listening development are directly proportional to the quantity of time spent in focused listening. By focused listening, I mean listening for specific aspects of the musical performance. Given the focus of this text, the conductor can greatly improve rehearsal skills by focusing solely on matters of choral texture and color as heard through critical listening to vowel shapes and colors.

In the second section of this chapter, I make specific recommendations. For initial further study, I highly recommend the Resource Recordings for *Teaching Music through Performance in Choir, Volume 1* featuring The Westminster Williamson Voices, which I conduct, and the University of North Texas Chamber Choir, with Jerry McCoy conducting, distributed by GIA Publications (CD-650). One of the difficulties in recommending this type of aural study is the challenge of tracking down all the recordings necessary. This exceptional recording is also particularly useful because it contains twenty works as I conducted them, which allows you to clearly hear textural differences as dictated by my musical style.

Before You Listen:
The Sound Concept of The Westminster Williamson Voices

Before you listen to this recording, I need to state several things up front. I can only speak about the sound of the choir I conduct. Jerry McCoy's choir sings beautifully, and, knowing him, he has biases about tone as do I. I will comment here only on my biases with respect to the choir I conduct.

While many believe that there is a characteristic "Westminster Sound," that statement is very far from the truth. Since the founding of the college, the ensemble sound of the institution has been a reflection of all those who teach there. Influences are very strong in one's "textural" life. Frauke Haasemann, Wilhelm Ehmann, and Elaine Brown did much to bias my ears. The sounds heard on this recording are all results of what I believe to be an on-the-breath sound. Singers are encouraged to sing, and matters of blend are handled totally by seating position, because the seating position is central to both hearing and sound.

Also, considerable care is taken to adequately close vowels to achieve good pitch. Aside from closing the vowel, vowel closure maintains the "oo" or head tone in the choral sound. One other important factor that has strongly influenced the timbre of the choir is the intensive work that the choir does with Harmonic Immersion Solfege. All pieces are learned on solfege with closed vowels so that pitch accuracy is of primary importance in the initial stages of learning a piece. Also, as I stated earlier, all the recordings were recorded as the choir rehearses, i.e., with altos in the first row, sopranos in the second row, basses in the third row, and tenors in the back row. I believe that this seating arrangement has a marked effect on the timbre of the ensemble.

Section Eight: Recommended Listening List for Further Aural Analysis and Color Study

Recommended Track Listening from Resource Recordings to *Teaching Music through Performance in Choir, Volume 1*

Title/Composer: Be Thou My Vision, arr. Alice Parker
Track: Disc 1, Track 1
Vowel Shape: Round
Comments: While the majority of this recording demonstrates a round choral resonance, one can hear a decidedly different resonance used during the soprano descant in the last verse of the piece. The resonance in the soprano is tall and narrow.

Title/Composer: Old Abram Brown, *Benjamin Britten*
Track: Disc 1, Track 3
Vowel Shape: Tall/narrow
Comments: This is one of the best examples of a tall, narrow resonance. An attempt was also made to further slenderize the resonance through use of British English. One should listen closely for the amount of vowel closure used to achieve this tall, narrow resonance. Because of the frequent singing in octaves, it was necessary to maintain a tall/narrow sound through vowel closure.

Title/Composer: Ave verum corpus, *Edward Elgar*
Track: Disc 1, Track 5
Vowel Shape: Tall/narrow
Comments: Latin sung with a British "style" is employed on this recording. To accomplish this, Italianate Latin vowels are produced from a tall, narrow perspective. On specific pitches where intonation could be problematic, vowels are more closed.[1]

Title/Composer: El Grillo, *Josquin des Prez*
Track: Disc 1, Track 7
Vowel Shape: Round
Comments: Round vowels are used on this recording. An effort was made to bring the round vowels more high and forward to "brighten" the color of the piece and to reflect the spirit of the text.

---

1. Information on how to instruct the choir to sing "closed" or "open" vowels can be found in *The Choral Warm-Up*.

Title/Composer: Psallite, *Michael Praetorius*
Track: Disc 1, Track 9
Vowel Shape: Tall/narrow
Comments: A tall, narrow approach to the vowel is used in this piece to help bring out the contrapuntal textures.

Title/Composer: Ave verum corpus, *Wolfgang A. Mozart*
Track: Disc 1, Track 11
Vowel Shape: Tall/narrow
Comments: Tall, narrow vowels are employed on this selection. A high and forward placement is also employed. This is necessary for Mozart that allows for more "spin" in the vocal line.

Title/Composer: Bogoróditse Djévo, *Arvo Pärt*
Track: Disc 1, Track 12
Vowel Shape: Round
Comments: This piece poses many diction challenges for any choir. Proper vowel color is paramount to the effective performance of this piece. This piece represents one of the roundest vowel resonances of any work on this recording.

Title/Composer: Circus Band, *Charles Ives*
Track: Disc 1, Track 14
Vowel Shape: Round, tall/narrow
Comments: Two contrasting choral resonances are used on this recording. For the unison sections of the piece, a tall/narrow approach to the vowel is employed. However, in the SATB sections, the sound of the choir changes to a round vowel approach. The contrast between resonances works very effectively in this work.

Title/Composer: Dirait-on, *Morten Lauridsen*
Track: Disc 1, Track 15
Vowel Shape: Tall/narrow
Comments: Extremely tall and narrow vowel resonances are employed in this recording, combined with liquid consonants. Musical ideas carried on the tall narrow vowel stream always conclude on the end of phrase lines. A conscious musical attempt is made to maintain all

Section Eight: Recommended Listening List for Further Aural Analysis and Color Study

resonential characteristics of the French language. French nasals were brought more forward because of the nature of the choral texture.

Title/Composer: He, Watching over Israel, *Felix Mendelssohn*
Track: Disc 1, Track 20
Vowel Shape: Round, tall/narrow
Comments: Mendelssohn presents particular performance issues for the choral conductor. If the sound is too round, musical lines do not move forward. If the sound is too tall and narrow, the warmth of sound inherent in the music of Mendelssohn is lost. An appropriate balance between these two resonances must be sought to arrive at a color that is musically appropriate. Use a tall, narrow resonance, with some added roundness of vowels for additional resonential color.

Title/Composer: Notre Père, *Maurice Duruflé*
Track: Disc 2, Track 7
Vowel Shape: Tall/narrow
Comments: As in the Lauridsen work on this recording, tall, narrow vowels and liquid consonants that bring no undue weight upon the musical line are employed.

Title/Composer: Salmo 150, *Ernani Aguiar*
Track: Disc 2, Track 8
Vowel Shape: Tall/narrow
Comments: This piece features the most tall and narrow choral resonance that can be heard on this recording. Because of the harmonic language of the conductor, it is necessary for the most tall/narrow resonance to be used, especially in the women's parts.

Title/Composer: Set Me as a Seal, *René Clausen*
Track: Disc 2, Track 9
Vowel Shape: Round
Comments: The interpretation of this piece reaches for a choral sound characteristic of the honesty, simplicity, and inherent humility and love exemplified by the text. The warmth of the human statement by each singer determines the color of this performance.

Title/Composer: Shenandoah, *arr. James Erb*
Track: Disc 2, Track 10
Vowel Shape: Round
Comments: Round vowels are used in this piece. Minimized diphthongs greatly enhance the sound of this work. Very closed round vowels in the final bars of the piece achieve the appropriate color for the *piano* dynamic. In eight-part textures, an attempt was made to use slightly taller and narrower vowels in the bass and baritone parts to enhance both the color and the resonance of the piece.

Title/Composer: Sicut cervus, *Palestrina*
Track: Disc 2, Track 11
Vowel Shape: Tall/narrow
Comments: Because of the contrapuntal nature of this work and the sound ideal of Palestrina, tall/narrow vowels are employed throughout.

Title/Composer: Sure on This Shining Night, *Samuel Barber*
Track: Disc 2, Track 12
Vowel Shape: Round
Comments: Round vowels are employed throughout this work. This piece uses one of the roundest resonances employed by this choir on this recording along with the Moses Hogan spiritual.

Title/Composer: Wade in the Water, *arr. Moses Hogan*
Track: Disc 2, Track 14
Vowel Shape: Round
Comments: This is another example of the most round and resonant vowel used to achieve a richness of choral color.[2]

---

[2]. It should be noted that issues of pitch will be problematic if some approach to "learning the piece in tune" is not employed in the rehearsal process. Solfege was used to anchor the intonation before text was added. Generally, it is a wiser decision to make sure the piece is in tune before adding the full qualities of rounder vowel resonances.

Section Eight: Recommended Listening List for Further Aural Analysis and Color Study

Title/Composer: Song of Peace, *Vincent Persichetti*
Track: Disc 2, Track 16
Vowel Shape: Tall/narrow
Comments: This work poses many musical challenges. Because the work is in phrygian, tuning is a serious issue that can only be approached and refined through tall/narrow vowels. Somewhat "extreme" vowel closures are employed on notes within the phrygian mode that pose tuning issues. "Eh" and "ih" vowels are sung more closed because of similar intonation issues. Particular note should be made on the color of the vowel sounds employed on the primary tune, which begins in the singers' lower register.

Supplementary Recordings Recommended for Further Aural Study

Title/Contents: *Blessed Spirit: Music of the Soul's Journey*. Gregorian chant, Gustav Holst, John Sheppard, Heinrich Schutz, Russian traditional, Sir Henry Walford Davies, and American Spirituals (Collegium).
Ensemble: The Choir of Clare College, Cambridge
Conductor: Timothy Brown
Vowel Shape: Tall/narrow and round
Comments: This is a wonderful recording because it presents a wide variety of choral ensemble colors in one package. I find the sound of Timothy Brown's choir to be flexible, resonant, and stylistically appropriate. Highly recommended.

Title: *Our American Journey* (Teldec)
Ensemble: Chanticleer
Vowel Shape: Tall/narrow
Title: Five Centuries of Choral Music (Clarion)
Ensemble: The Swedish Radio Choir
Conductor: Eric Ericson
Vowel Shape: Tall/narrow
Comments: This stunning recording should be in every musician's choral library. The recording covers five centuries of choral music. Despite the various musical styles, the choral sound remains within the realm of tall, narrow sounds.

Title: *Voices from a Sixteenth-Century Cathedral* (Angel)
Ensemble: The Roger Wagner Chorale
Conductor: Roger Wagner
Vowel Shape: Round
Comments: This recording presents the model for round, resonential sounds in choral music.

Title: *Maurice Duruflé: The Complete Music for Choir* (BIS CD-602)
Ensemble: St. Jacob's Chamber Choir
Conductor: Gary Garden
Vowel Shape: Tall/narrow
Comments: Without doubt, this is one of the most stunning recordings

Section Eight: Recommended Listening List for Further Aural Analysis and Color Study

of the choral music of Duruflé. While the choir sings with a beautifully focused and in-tune sound, their tone possesses warmth and flexibility. Vowel colors employed in this recording are exceptional.

Title/Contents: *Sacred and Profane* (Harmonia Mundi, HMC 901734)
Benjamin Britten, Edward Elgar, Frederick Delius, and Charles Stanford
Ensemble: RIAS Kammerchor
Conductor: Marcus Creed
Vowel Shape: Round bias
Comments: This wonderful choir, while it possesses a very lean sound, crosses the boundary slightly as far as choral tone is concerned. The ensemble maintains a stylistic integrity for this English music but adds a slightly rounder vowel shape to its production.

Title: *Rachmaninoff: Vespers* (Telarc)
Ensemble: Robert Shaw Festival Singers
Conductor: Robert Shaw
Vowel Shape: Round
Comments: This recording represents some of Shaw's most beautiful work. It is an invaluable recording for the study of round, resonant choral sounds.

Title: *Motets of the Romantic Era* (Cantate)
Ensemble: Westfalische Kantorei
Conductor: Wilhelm Ehmann
Vowel Shape: Round
Comments: Of all the recordings available, this is the one that demonstrates the ideal "romantic" sound. Although it is difficult to find, it is worth the effort.

Title: *Lauridsen: The Complete Choral Cycles* (Fresh Water Records, FWCL 105-2)
Ensemble: Choral Cross Ties
Conductor: Bruce Browne
Vowel Shape: Tall/narrow and round
Comments: This recording demonstrates an ensemble with a flexible sound concept that adapts to various styles of literature.

Title/Contents: *Illumina* (Collegium, COLCD 125) Gregorian chant, William Byrd, Hildegard von Bingen, and Alexander Grechaninov
Ensemble: The Choir of Clare College, Cambridge
Conductor: Timothy Brown
Vowel Shape: Tall/narrow and round
Comments: This CD is a particularly good resource because it presents not only a wide variety of styles but contrasting choral colors.

Title: *Tarik O'Regan: Voices* (Collegium, COLCD 130)
Ensemble: The Choir of Clare College, Cambridge
Conductor: Timothy Brown
Vowel Shape: Tall/narrow
Comments: This superb recording should be a must have for all conductors who are students of choral sound. Most noteworthy from a sound perspective on this recording is the consistently produced tall, narrow vowel sounds. On this recording, one should note the different "brighter" vowels in English-speaking choirs. Of particular note is the beautiful "ah" vowel of this choir. The recording also represents on-the-breath singing.

Title: *Love Is Spoken Here* (CFN 0507-2)
Ensemble: Mormon Tabernacle Choir
Conductor: Craig Jessop and Mack Wilberg
Vowel Shape: Round
Comments: This beautiful CD is a wonderful example of round sounds used to lyrical advantage, especially in the context of folk music. I highly recommend track 7. One should make note of the remarkable consistency of vowel sounds in this 300+ member choir.

Title: *A Ceremony of Carols** (Marquis 81327)[3]
Ensemble: The Toronto Children's Chorus
Conductor: Jean Ashworth Bartle
Vowel Shape: Tall/narrow
Comments: All conductors of children's choirs should use this

---

3. Asterisks denote a recording featuring children's choir.

Section Eight: Recommended Listening List for Further Aural Analysis and Color Study

recording as their benchmark of beautifully produced children's singing. The production on this recording is outstanding; vowel sounds are always resonant, free, and on the breath.

Title: *Light of the Spirit* (Collegium, CSACD 902)
Ensemble: The Choir of Clare College, Cambridge
Conductor: Timothy Brown
Vowel Shape: Varied
Comments: Of all the recordings recommended for further listening, this comes with my highest recommendation. The two-CD set covers all styles from Gregorian chant to Heinrich Schutz to Györgi Ligeti to Norman Luboff. There are few recordings that dare to tackle such a broad range of music styles. What is unique about this recording is that each composer is treated with stylistic integrity with regard to sound. This recording is a must-own for choral conductors.

Title: *Parish Anthems* (Gamut Recordings)
Ensemble: The Choir of Clare College, Cambridge
Conductor: Timothy Brown
Vowel Shape: Tall/narrow
Comments: The sounds on these traditional hymns, by and large, employ a relatively tall and narrow approach to singing. As always, the choral singing is exquisite and serves as a great aural model for conductors.

Title: *Dreams** (Ondine, ODE 786-2)
Ensemble: Tapiola Choir
Conductor: Erkki Pohjola, Osmo Vänskä
Vowel Shape: Tall/narrow
Comments: This is probably one of the most outstanding examples of what is achievable with children's voices. The vowel concept is remarkable for pitch clarity and color. Production is phenomenally consistent and at all times breathtaking.

Title: *The Angel Choir and the Trumpeter** (Eastern Mennonite University)
Ensemble: Shenandoah Valley Children's Choir
Conductor: Julia White
Vowel Shape: Tall/narrow

Comments: This recording of Christmas pieces with brass is an example of a natural children's sound with a consistent approach to vowel sound.

Title: *1994 England and Scotland Tour**
Ensemble: Indianapolis Children's Choir
Conductor: Henry Leck
Vowel Shape: Round
Comments: While it is dangerous at times to categorize sounds, the sounds on this recording are perhaps some of the most stunningly natural children's sounds that I have heard on any recording.

Title: *Hear through the Ages** (Mark Custom Recording, 3185-MCD)
Ensemble: Piedmont Choirs
Conductor: Robert Geary
Vowel Shape: Round
Comments: The works on this recording are representative of a rounder approach to resonance applied to a children's choir, used with great artistry.

Title: *Untraveled Worlds** (Pelagos International, PEL 1004)
Ensemble: Chorus Angelicus
Conductor: Paul Halley
Vowel Shape: Tall/narrow
Comments: This beautiful recording is another for resonance study. The sound is open, free, and resonant. There is also appropriate variation in between styles. This recording is a beautiful model. Of particular note is the recording of Orlando Gibbons's "Drop, Drop Slow Tears."

Title: *My Heart Soars** (Marquis Classics, ERAD 199)
Ensemble: Toronto Children's Chorus
Conductor: Jean Ashworth Bartle
Vowel Shape: Tall/narrow
Comments: The remarkably consistent and beautiful sound of the Toronto Children's Chorus is presented on this exquisite recording through a variety of musical styles. Of special note is the singing of the sopranos. Vowel concepts on this recording are worth studying. Bartle achieves a remarkable legato.

Section Eight: Recommended Listening List for Further Aural Analysis and Color Study

Title: *Closing the Century** (Amabile, AM 0020 2231)
Ensemble: Jitro Czech Children's Chorus
Conductor: Jiri Skopal
Vowel Shape: Tall/narrow
Comments: This recording is a stunning example of a children's choir singing with a consistent resonance concept applied to varied choral literature. Vowel concepts on this recording are particularly noteworthy.

Title: *2002 Spring Concert**
Ensemble: St. Louis Children's Chorus
Conductor: Barbara Berner
Vowel Shape: Round
Comments: Of all the recordings suggested on this list, it is perhaps the sound that comes closest to my personal biases concerning tone in children's choirs. The conductor elicits exquisitely natural vocal production with a consistent approach to vowels, all supported with a remarkable honesty of expression within the tone. I highly recommend this recording.

Other Suggested Recordings

49 Hidden Treasures from The African American Heritage Hymnal, dir. James Abbington, GIA Publications, Inc. (CD-636).

Arvo Pärt: De Profundis. The Theater of Voices dir. Paul Hilyer, Harmonia Mundi 907182.

The Cambridge Singers Collection, The Cambridge Singers dir. John Rutter, Collegium.

The Complete Bach Motets, The Westminster Choir dir. Wilhelm Ehmann.

Eric Ericson Conducts Virtuoso Choral Music (Reger, Strauss, Penderecki, Messiaen, Martin), Rundfunkchor Stockholm and the Stockholmer Kammerchor, Clarion CLR 902CD.

Hymn, The American Boychoir dir. James Litton, Angel Records.

John Tavener: Ikon of Light (Funeral Ikos, The Lamb), The Tallis Scholars, Gimell CDGIM 005.

Kleine Geistliche Konzerte, dir. Wilhelm Ehmann, Cantate C 57606.

Mendelssohn: Elijah, The Singing City Choir and the Philadelphia Orchestra dir. Eugene Ormandy.

Messe cum jubilo, Duruflé, Festival Singers of Loyola Marymount University dir. Paul Salamunovich, Loyola Marymount University.

Resources

Blocker, Robert, ed. *The Robert Shaw Reader*. New Haven: Yale University Press, 2004.

Buchanan, Heather, and James Jordan. *Evoking Sound Video: Body Mapping Principles and Basic Conducting Technique*. Chicago: GIA, 2002.

Bunch, Meribeth. *Dynamics of the Singing Voice*. New York: Springer-Verlag, 1982.

Conable, Barbara. *What Every Musician Needs to Know about the Body: The Practical Application of Body Mapping to Making Music*. Portland, OR: Andover Press, 2000. (Distributed by GIA Publications.)

Decker, Harold A., and Julius Herford. *Choral Conducting Symposium*. Englewood Cliffs, NJ: Prentice Hall, 1988.

Gordon, Edwin E. *Instrument Timbre Preference Test*. Chicago: GIA Publications, 1984. (G-2830K)

———. *Learning Sequences in Music: Skill, Content, and Patterns* (2003 Edition). Chicago: GIA Publications, 2003.

———. *Preparatory Audiation, Audiation, and Music Learning Theory: A Handbook of a Comprehensive Music Learning Sequence*. Chicago: GIA Publications, 2001.

Jordan, James, and Marilyn Shenenberger. *Ear Training Immersion Exercises for Choirs*. Chicago: GIA Publications, 2004.

Madaule, Paul. *When Listening Comes Alive: A Guide to Effective Learning and Communication*. Norval, Ontario: Moulin Publishing, 1993.

Rothko, Mark. *The Artist's Reality: Philosophies of Art*. New Haven: Yale University Press, 2004.

Shafir, Rebecca Z. *The Zen of Listening: Mindful Communication in the Age of Distraction*. Wheaton, IL: Quest Books, 2003.

Tomatis, Alfred. *The Conscious Ear: My Life of Transformation through Listening*. Barrytown, NY: Station Hill Press, 1991.

———. *The Ear and the Voice*. Translated by Roberta Prada and Pierre Sollier. Freely adapted by Roberta Prada and Francis Keeping. Lanham, MD: Scarecrow Press, 2005.

Biographies

James Jordan is recognized and praised from many quarters in the musical world as one of the nation's preeminent conductors, writers, and innovators in choral music. He has been called a "visionary" by the *Choral Journal*. His career and publications have been devoted to innovative educational changes in the choral art that have been embraced around the world. A master teacher, Jordan's pioneering writing and research concerning the use of Laban Movement Analysis for the teaching of conducting and movement to children has dramatically changed teaching in both those disciplines. Called the "Father of the Case Study," he was the first researcher to bring forward the idea of the case study as a viable and valuable form of research for the training and education of teachers.

One of the country's most prolific writers on the subjects of the philosophy of music making and choral teaching, he has produced ten major textbooks and several choral series bearing his name. His recent publications include *Learn to Conduct Using the Swiss Exercise Ball: Developing Kinclusive Conducting Awareness*, *Ear Training Immersion Exercises for Choirs: Choral Exercises in All the Modes* (book, CD, and singer's edition), *Evoking Sound: The Choral Warm-Up, Core Vocal Exercises* (book, CD, and accompanist supplement), and *The Musician's Walk* (all published by GIA Publications).

His books on the subject of vocal technique for choirs are considered essential pedagogical tools. His choral conducting book *Evoking Sound: Fundamentals of Choral Conducting and Rehearsing* was named as a "must read" by the *Choral Journal*. His text *Ear Training Immersion Exercises for Choirs*, details the first comprehensive approach toward aural literacy for choirs using Harmonic Immersion Solfege™ and a unique system of score analysis that focuses upon the aural perceptions of the choir. His trilogy of books, *The Musician's Soul*, *The Musician's Spirit*, and *The Musician's Walk*, have been acclaimed by both instrumental and choral conductors alike and have been credited with humanizing music education.

Jordan also serves as Executive Editor of the Evoking Sound Choral Series published by GIA. This series presents choral literature at the highest levels for high school and college choirs. In addition to new compositions by America's finest composers, the series also presents expert editions of standard choral repertoire. Also unique to this series are solfege editions that use Jordan's groundbreaking approach to the use of solfege in choral ensembles with accurate aural analysis as the basis of the approach.

Jordan teaches and conducts at the Westminster Choir College of Rider University in Princeton, New Jersey, one of the foremost centers for the study and performance of choral music in the world, where he is an associate professor of conducting and senior conductor. For the past twelve years, he has served as conductor of The Westminster Chapel Choir. In fall 2004, he founded one of Westminster's highly select touring and performing choirs, The Westminster Williamson Voices. This choir's mission, beyond choral performance and recording at the highest levels, is to serve as an ensemble that employs cutting-edge approaches to the choral rehearsal and choral performance. The ensemble specializes in premiering significant contributions to choral literature. The choir has championed the new works of Jackson Hill, Roger Ames, Tarik O'Regan, Gerald Custer, and Brian Schmidt. The ensemble has also collaborated in performances with The Spiral Q Puppet Theater (Philadelphia) and Archedream Dance Theater (www.archedream.com). The Westminster Williamson Voices is featured on the CD set for *Teaching Music through Performance in Choir*, Volume 1, Levels 1–3 (GIA CD-650). During the 2004–05 academic year, Jordan was also Visiting Distinguished Professor of Music Education at West Chester State University.

Jordan has had the privilege of studying with several of the landmark teachers of the twentieth century. He was a student of Elaine Brown, Wilhelm Ehmann, and Frauke Haasemann. He completed his PhD in the psychology of music under Edwin E. Gordon. James Jordan has been the recipient of many awards for his contributions to the profession. He was named Distinguished Choral Scholar at the University of Alberta and was made an honorary member of Phi Mu Alpha Sinfonia in 2002 at Florida State University. Composer Morten Lauridsen dedicated a movement of his acclaimed *Mid-Winter Songs* to him.

Jordan's writings and professional activities are detailed on his Web site, www.evokingsound.com. A comprehensive listing of his workshops, seminars, and publications can be found at www.giamusic.com/jordan.

Marilyn Shenenberger has worked closely with James Jordan at Westminster Choir College for the past three years as both a musical and pedagogical partner. She has been an integral part of Jordan's work in teaching Choral Ensemble Intonation. Shenenberger has provided aural awareness accompaniments for Jordan's Chapel Choirs, which are featured on *Choral Ensemble Intonation: Teaching Procedures Video* and has presented these concepts as a clinician at seminars and summer workshops. Shenenberger's accompaniments are included in Jordan's book *The Choral Warm-Up: Method, Procedures, and Core Vocal Exercises*. She received her master's degree in choral conducting from Westminster Choir College; holds a Dalcroze certificate from the Dalcroze School of Music in Manhattan, where she studied under Robert Abramson, Anne Farber, and Ruth Alperson; and completed her music education training at Lebanon Valley College. She is a seasoned performer and has worked collaboratively with a variety of vocal and instrumental soloists and choral ensembles in the United States and in Europe, most recently accompanying for cellist Robert Cafaro of the Philadelphia Orchestra. In addition to accompanying and performing chamber music, Shenenberger is the director of music at Faith United Presbyterian Church in Medford, New Jersey, where she is the organist and director of three handbell choirs, a children's choir, two youth choirs, and an adult choir.

The Westminster Williamson Voices is composed of students at Westminster Choir College of Rider University. Emphasizing world music and the music of our time, it is named for Westminster's founder, John Finley Williamson, who believed that choral music performed at the highest level should be accessible to all so as to communicate the human essence that is at the heart of choral singing.

The select forty-voice ensemble combines choral performance with educational outreach, artistic collaborations, and partnering with other art forms, such as dance, theater, and the visual arts. Recent seasons have included performances of Eric Whitacre's *Leonardo Dreams of His Flying Machine* with Philadelphia's Spiral Q Puppet Theater and Gian Carlo Menotti's *The Unicorn, Gorgon and Manticore* with the Archedream Dance Theater, also of Philadelphia.

Serving as a living choral laboratory, the primary musical mission of The Westminster Williamson Voices is to explore new methods of teaching and rehearsing and to be at the forefront of choral education pedagogy. The ensemble uses contemporary ensemble methods involving the groundbreaking Aural Immersion Solfege™ and movement pedagogy, emphasizing the philosophies of both Dalcroze and Laban as well as exploring new avenues for the art of choral accompanying. The accompanist for the ensemble assumes a new role, becoming the keystone for aural training for the choir. Consequently, its members gain valuable pedagogical tools to use in their life's work as teachers and professional singers.

Westminster Choir College of Rider University is a center for music studies located in the heart of Princeton, New Jersey. At Westminster's core is a four-year music college and graduate school that prepares men and women for careers as music leaders in schools, universities, churches, and professional and community organizations.

The major programs of study are distinctly career oriented, leading to bachelor and master of music degrees as well as a bachelor of arts degree in music. Programs include music education; music theater; music theory and composition; sacred music; voice, organ, and piano performance and pedagogy; choral conducting; piano accompanying and coaching; and arts administration. In addition, Westminster offers two summer-study programs: Master of Music Education and Master of Voice Pedagogy.

In addition to The Westminster Williamson Voices, the college has seven major choirs, including the 150-voice Westminster Symphonic Choir, which has performed and recorded with virtually all of the major orchestras and conductors of our time.

Westminster also serves amateur and professional musicians through an extensive continuing education program that includes one-day Saturday seminars and one-week summer session programs. It also offers thirteen different summer programs for high school and middle school students.

Celebrating more than eighty years of musical excellence, Westminster Choir College of Rider University has significantly influenced the cultural life of our nation. It has been estimated that each week, Westminster graduates conduct and teach more than one million musicians worldwide.

Rider University, a private coeducational university with campuses in Lawrenceville and Princeton, New Jersey, emphasizes purposeful connections between academic study and education for the professions. Its four colleges—College of Business Administration; College of Liberal Arts,

Education, and Sciences; College of Continuing Studies; and Westminster Choir College—provide dynamic undergraduate programs in more than sixty areas and graduate programs in eighteen specialties.

The Pennsbury High School Choral Music Department is composed of seven choirs spanning grades nine through twelve, involving a total of more than five hundred students. The department includes the auditioned **Chamber Choir** and a four-level music theory program, and presents two annual musical theatre productions. Five staff persons from varied backgrounds team-teach ensembles and classes within the department.

Members of the Chamber Choir are selected from the program's tenth, eleventh, and twelfth grade students through competitive auditions. Repertoire is selected each year from accompanied and *a cappella* music of many centuries. The choir rehearses after school two to three days per week and performs at a wide variety of school and community functions. The choir also tours annually, most recently traveling to England, Wales, and Ireland in April 2006. The choir has performed abroad in such venues as St. Patrick's Cathedral and St. Mary's Pro-Cathedral in Dublin, Ireland; St. David's Cathedral in St. David, Wales; Tabernacle Church and Tesco Stage of the Wales Millennium Centre in Cardiff, Wales; and St. Mary Abbot's Church in London. In the U.S., the choir has sung at The White House, Carnegie Hall, the Washington National Cathedral, and Fenway Park. The choir has worked under many noted conductors in the recent past, including James Jordan, Donald Nally, Donald Dumpson, Ann Howard Jones, John Guthmiller, and Joseph Flummerfelt.

Recently the choir presented the U.S. premiere of Carl Heinrich Graun's *Weihnachts-Oratorium*, a recently reconstructed Baroque masterwork with guest orchestra and soloists. The choir participated in the Pennsbury Bernstein Festival, a three-day celebration highlighting the choral music of Leonard Bernstein. The composer's son, Alexander, served as guest speaker for the event. The choir also was highlighted in the much-acclaimed Pennsbury Welsh Music Festival, a four-day series of concerts and presentations featuring the choral music of Wales. Composer Meuryn Hughes of Cardiff, Wales, and baritone Leon Williams were in residence for the duration of the festival, which culminated in the second U.S. performance of *Dewi Sant* (St. David) by Wales' most celebrated composer, Arwel Hughes.

James D. Moyer, a native of Easton, Pennsylvania, is the director of choral activities at Pennsbury High School and the curriculum coordinator for vocal/choral music (K–12) for the Pennsbury School District located in lower Bucks County, Pennsylvania. Prior to his appointment at Pennsbury, he was director of choral activities at Western Branch High School in Chesapeake, Virginia.

Moyer also serves as the director of music and fine arts for the First Presbyterian Church in Morrisville, Pennsylvania, and is cofounder and music director of the Pennsbury Community Chorus. He is a former ACDA State President (Virginia), has served on several national and divisional convention committees, and has written choral music, choral recording, and book reviews for the *Choral Journal*.

A sought-after clinician, adjudicator, and guest conductor, Moyer most recently served as an adjudicator for the University of Mississippi Choral Festival and was a guest conductor for the Westminster Choir College Summer Vocal Institute in Princeton. His choirs have sung in major venues across the world, including the Forty-first Spoleto Festival in Spoleto, Italy, at the direct invitation of composer Gian Carlo Menotti.

Moyer holds degrees from Westminster Choir College (bachelor of music) and the University of Oklahoma (master of music in choral conducting). His principal teachers have included Frauke Haasemann, Allen Crowell, Joseph Flummerfelt, Dennis Shrock, and James Jordan. He resides in Yardley, Pennsylvania, with his wife, soprano Kathryn Thomas Moyer, and son, James.

Jason D. Vodicka graduated *summa cum laude* from Westminster Choir College with a bachelor of music degree in music education and voice in 2002. While at Westminster he was a member of the world-renowned Westminster Choir and the Westminster Symphonic Choir, performing as a chorister with the New York Philharmonic, Royal Concertgebouw (Amsterdam), New Jersey Symphony, and the Spoleto Festival (USA) Orchestra. He also accompanied the college's Symphonic Choir, Chapel Choir, Vocal Institute, and Schola Cantorum at the keyboard in numerous rehearsals and performances. He is privileged to have accompanied conducting master classes with Joseph Flummerfelt, Dennis Keene, and Robert Page, who were named by the *New York Times* as three successors to the Robert Shaw legacy. He is a featured organist on Westminster's recording "An Evening of Readings and Carols" and played for these annual performances for four years in the Princeton University Chapel. He is also featured on *Hymnos*, a recording of hymns for brass and organ by the Mainstreet Brass.

Currently, Vodicka is employed as one of three choral directors at Pennsbury High School in lower Bucks County, Pennsylvania, where he conducts the 100-voice Chorale, codirects the select Chamber Choir, and produces an annual musical theatre production. Additionally, he is the incoming vice president of the Bucks County Music Educators Association. He accompanies the seventy-five-voice Pennsbury Community Chorus and leads voice-building and diction work for their performances of major choral works. For six years, Vodicka was principal organist at the First Presbyterian Church of Morrisville, Pennsylvania, where he also directed the church handbell program.

Vodicka has studied voice with Scott McCoy, organ with Stefan Engels, and conducting with James Jordan at the college level. Vodicka is the 2005 winner of the William Nash Scholarship, given by PMEA, toward his master's degree in music education from Westminster. Vodicka is a proud native of Raleigh, North Carolina, and currently resides in Morrisville, Pennsylvania in a 200-year-old historic home.

John C. Baker, recording engineer/producer, earned a bachelor of arts and a master of business administration from Rutgers University. His choral CD credits include the Westminster Choir, the St. Olaf College Choir, the Washington National Cathedral, the American Boychoir, and Princeton University, among many others. He has recorded projects throughout the United States, the United Kingdom, and continental Europe, in venues from Carnegie Hall, St. Paul's Cathedral, and Westminster Abbey in London to Berlin's Schauspielhaus and the Berliner Dome, Thomas Kirche in Leipzig, and the Moscow Conservatory and the Kappella in St. Petersburg. Labels for which he has engineered recordings include Great Britain's Linn and Avie labels, some of which have been released in the Sony Super Audio CD (SACD) 5.1 surround sound format. He has worked with James Jordan at Westminster Choir College for nearly a decade.